EXERCISE & PHYSICAL FITNESS

Gary A. Klug
Janice Lettunich

WELLNESS

A MODERN
LIFE-STYLE
LIBRARY

The Dushkin Publishing Group, Inc./Sluice Dock, Guilford, CT 06437

PO 99011091
22/6/99

The authors wish to dedicate this book to the memory of Professor Jan Broekhoff of the Department of Physical Education of the University of Oregon. Jan was a man who enriched our lives as a mentor, a teacher, and a colleague by demonstrating that he truly understood the meaning and significance of educating the body as well as the mind. He taught us and all those around him the true meaning of courage and integrity in the face of adversity.

Copyright © 1992 by The Dushkin Publishing Group, Inc., Guilford, Connecticut 06437. All rights reserved. No part of this book may be reproduced, stored, or otherwise transmitted by any means–mechanical, electronic, or otherwise–without written permission from the publisher.

Library of Congress Catalog Card Number: 91-057935
Manufactured in the United States of America
First Edition, First Printing
ISBN: 0-87967-871-2

Library of Congress Cataloging-in-Publication Data

Klug, Gary A., Exercise & physical fitness (Wellness)
    1. Exercise. 2. Physical fitness. I. Lettunich, Janice. II. Title.
III. Series.
GV461   613.71   91-057935   ISBN 0-87967-871-2

Please see page 157 for credits.

The procedures and explanations given in this publication are based on research and consultation with medical and nursing authorities. To the best of our knowledge, these procedures and explanations reflect currently accepted medical practice; nevertheless, they cannot be considered absolute and universal recommendations. For individual application, treatment suggestions must be considered in light of the individual's health, subject to a doctor's specific recommendations. The authors and the publisher disclaim responsibility for any adverse effects resulting directly or indirectly from the suggested procedures, from any undetected errors, or from the reader's misunderstanding of the text.

GARY KLUG

Gary Klug is an associate professor at the University of Oregon where his research deals with the cellular basis of muscle fatigue. Professor Klug received bachelor's and master's degrees in physical education from the University of Wisconsin-LaCrosse and a Ph.D. in the physiology of exercise from Washington State University. His professional career has included 5 years of teaching in the Appleton, Wisconsin, public school system and research positions in both the Department of Pharmacology at Southwestern Medical Center in Dallas, Texas, and in the Department of Biology at the University of Konstanz in Konstanz, Germany, where he was a Fellow of the Alexander von Humbolt Foundation. He became an assistant professor in the Department of Kinesiology at the University of Colorado in Boulder in 1983 before moving to his current position in 1985.

JANICE LETTUNICH

Janice Lettunich received a master's degree in physical education with emphasis in exercise physiology from the University of Oregon in 1985 where she became a member of the faculty of the Department of Exercise and Movement Science. She is certified by the American College of Sports Medicine as both a preventive/rehabilitative exercise specialist and a preventive/rehabilitative exercise test technologist. For several years she has worked as a cardiac rehabilitation therapist. Ms. Lettunich is currently a research assistant in the Human Performance Laboratory at the University of Texas at Austin while working toward a doctorate in clinical exercise physiology.

WELLNESS:
A Modern Life-Style Library

General Editors
Robert E. Kime, Ph.D.
Richard G. Schlaadt, Ed.D.

Authors
Paula F. Ciesielski, M.D.
Randall R. Cottrell, Ed.D.
Judith S. Hurley, M.S., R.D.
James K. Jackson, M.D.
Robert E. Kime, Ph.D.
Gary A. Klug, Ph.D.
David C. Lawson, Ph.D.
Janice Lettunich, M.S.
James D. Porterfield
Richard St. Pierre, Ph.D.
Richard G. Schlaadt, Ed.D.

Developmental Staff
Irving Rockwood, Program Manager
Paula Edelson, Series Editor
Lisa M. Clyde, Developmental Editor
Wendy Connal, Administrative Assistant
Jason J. Marchi, Editorial Assistant

Editing Staff
John S. L. Holland, Managing Editor
Catherine G. Leonard, Copy Editor
Diane Barker, Editorial Assistant
Mary L. Strieff, Art Editor
Robert Reynolds, Bob Italiano, Illustrators

Production and Design Staff
Brenda S. Filley, Production Manager
Whit Vye, Cover Design and Logo
Jeremiah B. Lighter, Text Design
Libra Ann Cusack, Typesetting Supervisor
Charles Vitelli, Designer
Meredith Scheld, Graphics Assistant
Steve Shumaker, Graphics Assistant
Lara M. Johnson, Graphics Assistant
Juliana Arbo, Typesetter
Richard Tietjen, Editorial Systems Analyst

I N THE LAST QUARTER CENTURY, a doctor's standard physical examination has included the advice to exercise regularly—and with good reason, for regular exercise is a vital tool in a wellness life-style. Information linking exercise to longevity, mental health, prevention of disease, increased energy, and a better outlook on life is growing. Unfortunately, our steadily increasing understanding of the importance of exercise has not been matched by a desire to put our knowledge into practice. Despite the much-publicized fitness boom of recent years, the life-style of most Americans is sedentary.

One of the purposes of this book, therefore, is to tempt you into exercising. There are very few people who cannot find at least one mode of exercise that is both practical and appealing. But once you have decided to start an exercise regimen, you will find yourself bombarded with questions that need answers if you are to make exercise a permanent part of your life-style. What precisely are your exercise goals? What form of exercise should you pursue to meet them? How often should you exercise? How can you monitor your progress accurately? How is exercise changing your body? In attempting to answer these questions, you may find yourself deluged with information, some of it more credible than the rest. Like nutrition or weight control, exercise is a subject that has generated a stream of often confusing and contradictory claims. And so the purpose of this book is to provide an information framework that can help you sort through these questions, claims, and counterclaims. The goals of *Exercise & Physical Fitness* are: (1) to identify and describe the benefits, both physical and mental, of regular exercise, (2) to help you undertand the importance of training and the differences among the various types of training, (3) to provide guidelines for exercising safely and effectively, (4) to identify common problems that cause people to drop out of their programs and strategies for overcoming them, and (5) to start you on your path of building an exercise program that will meet your desired goals.

Like the other volumes in this series, this is not a definitive work, but rather a place to begin. You should not expect to find a complete discussion of any one exercise topic. The central objective of this book is not to make you into an instant expert on exercise but to help you learn to *think critically* about this important topic. Only then will you be able to distinguish exercise myth from exercise fact, and only then will you be an informed health consumer.

Gary Klug
Janice Lettunich
Eugene, OR

Contents

1

Exercise and Life-Style

Page 1

2

Exercise, Fitness, and Training

Page 22

5

Types of
Exercise Programs

Page 83

FIGURES

TABLES

Exercise and Life-Style

"Living systems are worn out by inactivity and developed by use."

— A. Szent-Gyoryi

EXERCISE IS IN STYLE. Every day thousands of Americans work out with weights, run, attend aerobics classes, swim, bike, walk, or do other physical activities as part of their daily routines. Once reserved for professional athletes and a handful of fitness enthusiasts, **exercise** has become a part of many people's lives. A 1987 survey found, for example, that more than 23 million Americans were participating in an aerobics program, 66 million were swimming, 58 million were walking for exercise, and nearly 35 million were making regular use of some type of exercise equipment. [1] Health clubs, tennis courts, road races, and triathlons abound throughout the United States. Along with the increased popularity of exercise has come an enormous "fitness industry" which offers more than 40,000 health facilities of various sorts to an estimated 50 million exercise-hungry consumers. [2] Indeed, one of the biggest problems confronting the newcomer to exercise today is the need to choose from among a bewildering assortment of sports activities, exercise programs, and health and exercise equipment.

This upsurge of interest in exercise is a positive **life-style** trend, but it also raises some questions. Are people exercising for the right reasons? Are they exercising properly? Are they really

Exercise: Physical activity performed in order to improve or maintain one's fitness and/or increase caloric consumption.

Life-style: A way of living that consistently reflects a particular set of values and attitudes.

(continued on p. 3)

1

The 1980s was the decade of high-impact aerobics classes and high-mileage training. Yet there was something elitist about the way exercise was prescribed: *only* strenuous workouts would do, you *had* to raise your heart rate to between X and Y, the only way to go was to "go for the burn." And such strictures ensured that most "real" exercisers were relatively young and in good shape to begin with. Many, many Americans got caught up in the fitness boom, but probably just as many fell by the wayside.

Fitness Goes Democratic

What will the future be like for American exercise patterns and attitudes towards fitness? The trend is toward a more flexible, more democratic future that includes all sorts of health-giving exercise for people of all ages:

Being active is the key. . . . [R]ecent research shows that you don't have to run marathons to become fit—that burning just 1,000 calories a week in *moderate* exercise and daily activities (such as walking, gardening, and sports) is enough.

Anything goes, as long as it burns these calories. There will be more variety in activities. Aerobics classes and jogging will continue to attract exercisers, but as the nation and its fitness habits mature, people are shifting to gentler activities such as fitness walking, low-impact aerobics, and ballroom dancing. At the same time, others are choosing new types of strenuous sports, from mountain biking and rock climbing to biathlons and triathlons. They are also cross training—combining different (usually complementary) types of exercise to create a more rounded, less boring program. Step-aerobics is one innovative activity turning up at health clubs: it's like low-impact aerobic dance, except that participants step up and down on adjustable platforms, often holding light weights. Water aerobics also appears to be on the upswing.

Never too late. More and more studies are showing that exercise may inhibit, arrest, or even reverse many of the declines associated with aging. The most recent, published in June [1990] in the *Journal of the American Medical Association,* found that an eight-week weight-training program allowed frail 86- to 96-year-olds to build muscle mass and become more mobile and self-sufficient. (Older people who start exercising do have to take more time and work at a lower intensity to build cardiovascular and muscle strength.) As this message sinks in, we're likely to see more people in their sixties, seventies, and eighties starting to exercise. And it doesn't matter if you never really exercised before—the benefits will still accrue.

New technology. Every month there seems to be a new type of exercise equipment. There are recumbent exercise bikes and stair-climbing machines, and even computerized rowing machines that let you compete against a simulated rower on a video screen or that transport you to the Colorado River. Some weight machines even "read" your strength and provide the optimal resistance for you. There's little or no evidence that such high-price devices give you a better workout. But if your health club invests in high-tech exercise machines, they may make your workouts more fun and more varied— and thus help keep you motivated.

The whole body. Aerobic exercise such as running and cycling, which uses large muscle groups to enhance cardiovascular endurance, will continue to be the cornerstone of fitness programs, but there is likely to be a new emphasis on the other elements of fitness— overall muscle strength, flexibility, and agility. As people in long-term aerobic programs strengthen their hearts, they typically build up their leg muscles, but may lose muscle mass in their upper body. While a decade ago a very small proportion of women worked out with weights, a recent Gallup survey found that 15% of women who exercise regularly include weight training. The new interest in strengthening muscles is seen in the growing number of low-impact aerobics classes that utilize light hand weights.

A STRONG RECOMMENDATION

In order to provide a "well-rounded program," the American College of Sports Medicine recently altered its exercise guidelines—the first time in 12 years—to include strength training along with aerobic exercise for healthy adults. It recommends resistance training of *moderate* intensity at least twice a week: a minimum of 8 to 10 exercises involving the major muscle groups, each one repeated 8 to 12 times. This shouldn't be intimidating: it can take as little as 15 minutes per session. The resistance can be provided by barbells or weight machines. You can also use your own body weight as resistance, as in calisthenics such as push-ups, sit-ups, and pull-ups. Remember, too, that there's no set amount of weight you should lift and no standard against which you should measure yourself: the goal is to work out according to your capabilities.

Source: *University of California Berkeley Wellness Letter,* October 1990, p. 2.

Did You Know That . . .

Americans spent about $1.4 billion on home exercise machines in 1988.

any healthier as a result? Unfortunately, the answer to these questions is, "Not always." Too many enthusiastic exercisers are not realizing the full potential benefits of their efforts. In some cases, they may even be doing themselves harm by exercising too often (or not often enough), by trying to accomplish too much in too little time, or by following unsound or harmful advice. Most important, they may not be making the parallel changes in life-style—such as choosing nutritious foods and getting enough rest—necessary to realize the full range of health benefits from

FIGURE 1.1
Exercise Comes in Many Forms

CHOOSE YOUR WEAPON

Exercise is one of the best ways to help maintain a healthy heart. And it comes in many forms. Choose the one that fits you and put your heart in it.

Source: American Heart Association.

Many health organizations and groups endorse regular exercise as a means of improving or maintaining health.

any exercise program. The goal of any exercise program should be something more than just improving one's physical appearance. Exercise should be seen as an essential component of an entire **wellness** life-style.

THE SEDENTARY LIFE-STYLE AND ITS CONSEQUENCES

One reason for the fitness boom of recent years is our increased awareness of the unhealthy nature of a **sedentary** life-style. Unfortunately, such a life-style is typical of many Americans, for

Wellness: An approach to personal health that emphasizes the importance of a variety of behaviors in promoting health and preventing disease.

Sedentary: Accustomed to being physically inactive.

we live in a predominantly sedentary society. In large part, this is the result of technological progress. We have far more labor-saving devices, better medical treatment, and more leisure time than our great-grandparents did. Although generally positive, these developments also mean that most of us are far less physically active than were our ancestors. A 1987 study, for example, found that 60 percent of Americans are effectively "sedentary." [3] Each year we seem to spend more and more time sitting, whether at work, in school, in our cars, or at home in front of the television.

This decrease in activity has had negative effects on our health as a nation. As our lives have become more sedentary, we have become increasingly susceptible to what are sometimes referred to as the life-style diseases—diseases such as coronary heart disease and high blood pressure, which are among the leading causes of death in the United States (and most industrialized nations, for that matter). The single biggest killer in the United States today is **cardiovascular disease (CVD)**. It is estimated that more than 1 in 4 Americans currently suffers from some form of CVD. Each year, cardiovascular disease kills nearly 1 million Americans (175,000 under the age of 65), almost twice as many as the second leading cause of death—cancer—and nearly as many as all other causes of death in the United States combined. [4]

It is not just lack of physical activity that can increase the risk of cardiovascular disease. Another culprit is our modern way of life, which is continually becoming faster-paced, more complex, and more stressful. One result is an increased incidence of stress-related cardiovascular disease and other chronic diseases such as cancer, arthritis, and diabetes.

CARDIOVASCULAR DISEASE

The term cardiovascular disease actually refers to not one but several specific types of diseases that affect the heart and blood vessels. The most important of these are hypertension, coronary heart disease, rheumatic heart disease, and stroke.

Hypertension
Of these, the most common is **hypertension**, or high blood pressure. Hypertension is often called the silent killer because in most cases it produces few, if any, noticeable symptoms and therefore goes undetected. The American Heart Association esti-

---

Did You Know That . . .

Supervised walking programs serve as the main form of exercise in virtually every cardiac rehabilitation program in the world.

Cardiovascular disease (CVD): Any of several forms of disease of the heart and blood vessels.

Hypertension: Chronically high blood pressure that exceeds the level thought to be healthful.

FIGURE 1.2
Coronary Heart Disease

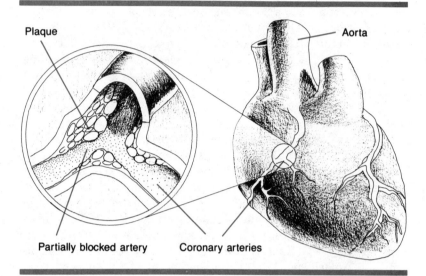

Plaque

Aorta

Partially blocked artery   Coronary arteries

Coronary heart disease occurs when plaque accumulates on the interior walls of the coronary arteries, reducing the flow of blood to the heart. If the arteries become too narrow to permit an adequate supply of blood to reach the heart, the result is a heart attack—sudden damage to one or more portions of the heart muscle.

mates that in 1988 (the latest figures available as of this writing) hypertension affected nearly 62 million Americans and caused nearly 31,000 deaths. [5] The causes of hypertension remain elusive, but it has been associated with obesity, smoking, and stress. [6] Some experts believe that high levels of dietary sodium (salt) intake are also a possible contributing factor, but this is unproven at the present time. Regardless of cause, untreated hypertension is a potentially serious condition that can lead to stroke, kidney disease, and heart failure.

Coronary Heart Disease

A less common but more dangerous form of cardiovascular disease is **coronary heart disease**. Coronary heart disease is the leading cause of death in the United States today, accounting for an estimated 511,050 deaths in the United States in 1988. [7] Coronary heart disease occurs when there is a reduction in the

Coronary heart disease:
Temporary or permanent damage to the heart muscle resulting from an insufficient flow of blood through the coronary arteries.

Effects of Exercise That May Help Prevent Heart Disease

- Decreases heart rate at rest and submaximal exercise
- Decreases systolic blood pressure at rest and submaximal exercise
- Decreases sympathetic nervous system tone
- Improves pump function of the heart
- Improves lipid (cholesterol and fat) profile
- Increases insulin sensitivity
- Decreases blood clot formation or increases clot removal
- Decreases obesity

Source: *Healthline*, Vol. 9, No. 7, July 1990, p. 15.

flow of blood through the major arteries supplying the heart (the **coronary arteries**).

The most frequent cause of coronary heart disease is **atherosclerosis**, which results from the accumulation of hard, fatty deposits called **plaque** on the walls of the coronary arteries. Over time, as the accumulation of plaque in the coronary arteries continues, the interior of the coronary arteries narrows and may, in severe cases, become completely blocked, thus restricting—or even completely shutting off—the flow of blood (and the supply of oxygen) to one or more portions of the heart. Unless this process is arrested or reversed, the eventual result is what is commonly known as a heart attack. (The technical term for heart attack is **myocardial infarction**.)

Researchers have identified at least three sets of risk factors that appear to be associated with cardiovascular disease. The first set consists of those factors that are essentially uncontrollable: sex, heredity, race, and age. The remaining two groups consist of factors over which we can exert some degree of control. The first of these, known as primary risk factors, includes three particularly important items: smoking, hypertension, and high levels of blood **cholesterol** and certain fatty proteins called **lipoproteins**. The remaining set, known as secondary risk factors, includes physical inactivity, diabetes, obesity, and stress. (See Table 1.1.) It should be emphasized that any effective strategy for reducing one's risk of cardiovascular disease must take both sets of controllable factors into account.

Coronary arteries: The arteries that supply blood to the heart muscle.

Atherosclerosis: A form of hardening of the arteries (arteriosclerosis) in which a substance known as plaque gradually accumulates on the interior of the artery walls, narrowing the arteries and reducing their elasticity.

Plaque: Fatty deposits that accumulate on arterial walls, restricting blood flow.

Myocardial infarction: The sudden death of a portion of the heart muscle; a heart attack.

Cholesterol: A fatlike substance found in food derived from animals and also manufactured by the body. It is essential to nerve and brain cell function, the synthesis of sex hormones, and is a component of bile acids used to aid fat digestion. Cholesterol is also part of the plaque that accumulates on artery walls as a result of atherosclerosis.

Lipoproteins: A class of proteins found in the blood that consist of a simple protein combined with a lipid (a fatty substance that is insoluble in the blood). They are transported throughout the body by the blood and are one of the body's important sources of food energy.

Table 1.1 Risk Factors for Heart Disease

Risk Factors Not Within Our Control:
Gender (Risk Greater in Men Than Women)
Family History (Risk Increases With Positive Family History)
Race (Risk Greater in Blacks)
Age (Risk Increases With Age)

Primary Risk Factors (Controllable to Some Extent):
Smoking
Hypertension
High Blood Cholesterol, LDL, or Total Cholesterol/HDL Ratio

Secondary Risk Factors (Controllable to Some Extent):
Diabetes
Physical Inactivity
Obesity
Stress

Source: *1991 Heart and Stroke Facts*, American Heart Association, pp. 20–21.

Researchers have identified three different sets of risk factors for cardiovascular disease. Two of these consist of factors that are wholly or partially within our control.

It is now widely accepted that there is an inverse relationship between level of physical activity and the incidence of cardiovascular disease. That is, a relatively low activity level increases the risk of cardiovascular disease and a relatively high activity level lowers it. Further, physical inactivity tends to compound the negative impact of other risk factors. Because of this, and because so many of us do lead sedentary lives, exercise is a critical component of any program to help prevent CVD. To be sure, exercise alone is not the entire answer. To be effective, an exercise program must be part of a broader effort that includes a range of appropriate life-style changes. If you are a smoker, for example, beginning an exercise program while continuing to smoke is taking halfway measures. An effective cardiovascular disease prevention program is one that addresses all known risk factors. Exercise should play a significant role in any such program.

Further, exercise is not just for adults. A number of studies have found evidence of widespread atherosclerosis among young people and even children, suggesting that the process begins much earlier than once was thought. [8] Adopting a suitable health maintenance program early in life can help avert severe health difficulties later on.

(continued on p. 10)

By now you've probably heard about the recently published study that presented the best evidence yet that exercise—more precisely, being fit and active—helps people live longer. You may have thought that you had heard this before. Why did this study make headlines when it was reported in the *Journal of the American Medical Association* in November [1989]?

One Small Step...

• It was the most extensive analysis yet of the effects of fitness on longevity, looking at more than 13,000 people for an average of eight years. The researchers, working at the Institute for Aerobics Research in Dallas, determined that all participants were in good health at the start of the study.

• It found that of the five groups of people, divided according to fitness levels, the least-fit group (who were also the most sedentary) had the highest mortality rates by far. The big surprise was that the death rate dropped most sharply in the second-least-fit group, by 60% for men and 48% for women. To be in this group, the researchers estimated, all a person would have to do is walk briskly for 30 to 60 minutes every day. The three fittest groups—including people who jogged up to 40 miles a week—derived relatively small additional benefits.

• It included women (more than 3,100 of them), who were found to benefit as much from being fit as the men. The few earlier studies of fitness in women were small and had ambiguous results.

• It evaluated subjects according to objective standards of fitness—the results of treadmill tests. In contrast, most earlier research relied on how much people said they exercised; such self-reports are likely to be unreliable.

• It suggested that being physically fit lowers the risk not only of heart disease (a well-established effect), but also cancer (for which there's less evidence) as well as all causes of death.

• It adjusted its data statistically to be sure that the higher mortality rate was due to lack of fitness and not other important risk factors, such as age, smoking, high cholesterol or blood pressure levels, and family history of heart disease. However, the researchers couldn't adjust for the fact that nearly all the participants were white and well-to-do.

As more than one expert noted, what this means is that you don't have to be a marathoner to greatly reduce your risks. If, like about 30% of Americans, you're largely sedentary and unfit, even modest increases in lower-intensity activities such as brisk walking may add years to your life. You still need to sweat a little, but not buckets.

Source: *University of California Berkeley Wellness Letter,* January 1990, p. 1.

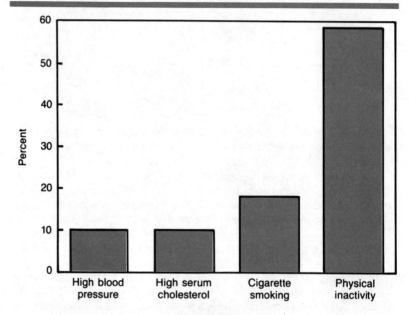

FIGURE 1.3
Fitness and the Risk of Coronary Heart Disease

Source: "Protective Effect of Physical Activity on Coronary Heart Disease," *Mortality and Morbidity Weekly Report*, Vol. 36, No. 26, 10 July 1987, p. 429.

More Americans are at risk for heart disease because of physical inactivity than because of any other manageable risk factor.

OBESITY AND OVERWEIGHT

Despite recent increases in the number of people who exercise, the United States is still a very fat society. There are an estimated 34 million or more Americans who are at least 20 percent over their ideal weight as determined by insurance company actuarial tables. [9] This does not include the many millions more who are less fat but whose weight still exceeds their ideal weight. Both groups have an increased risk of coronary heart disease. [10] They are also more likely to suffer from pulmonary and gall bladder diseases and certain types of cancer, and to die prematurely. [11]

Table 1.2 Weight-to-Mortality Relationship

Overweight (percent)	Excess Mortality* (percent)	
	Men	Women
10	13	9
20	25	21
30	42	30

*Compared with mortality of standard risks. Mortality ratio of standard risks equals 100%.

Source: Weight-to-Mortality Relationship, Metropolitan Life Insurance Company, derived from data of the Build and Blood Pressure Study, Society of Actuaries, 1979.

Being overweight can be fatal. The figures on the left are the percentages by which the individuals involved were overweight; the figures on the right are the excess mortality risk associated with these percentages. (All figures are the latest available.)

Why do we gain weight? At one level, the answer is simple. When we consume more fuel than we expend, measured in **calories**, the body converts the excess calories into fat. Because there are roughly 3,500 calories in a pound of fat, it follows that a person gains roughly 1 pound of additional body weight for every 3,500 calories consumed but not expended. This weight is stored in the body in the form of fat. Some of this fat, particularly that in certain organs and in portions of the nervous system, is **essential fat**. That is, it is critical to normal physiological functioning.

Another type of body fat is known as **storage fat**. This is fat stored in the body just under the skin surface and around various vital organs. A certain amount of storage fat is normal and (for a variety of reasons) also useful. However, too many of us are carrying more storage fat than we need. [12] People to whom this generalization applies are said to be overweight or obese. These individuals suffer from what may be termed an energy expenditure deficit. This deficit can occur whenever energy intake (in the form of food) is too great or energy expenditure (in the form of physical activity) is too small. In either case, the result is the same: an accumulation of energy stored as excess body fat. [13]

While excess weight clearly poses a serious health risk, defining terms like "overweight" and "obese" can be difficult. **Overweight** is usually defined as a weight in excess of an ideal weight as described by insurance company actuarial tables (see

Did You Know That . . .

People who watch television 3 or more hours a day are twice as likely to be obese as those who watch for less than an hour.

Calorie: The amount of heat energy required to raise the temperature of 1 gram of water 1 degree centigrade. The calories used in measuring the energy value of food are equivalent to 1,000 of these "small calories" and are, therefore, technically kilocalories (kcal), although in common usage we refer to them simply as calories.

Essential fat: Fat contained in various organs and portions of the nervous system that is essential to normal physiological functioning.

Storage fat: Fat in excess of the body's immediate energy needs that accumulates in layers beneath the skin and within and around various organs of the body.

Overweight: A somewhat elusive term that is usually used to describe individuals whose body weight exceeds by at least 20 percent the maximum amount recommended for their age, sex, height, and build in insurance company actuarial tables.

FIGURE 1.4
Caliper Testing of Body Fat

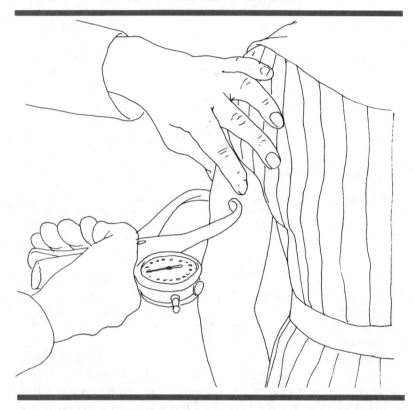

The percent of body fat can be estimated in a variety of ways. One of these involves using a pincer-type pair of calipers to measure skin thickness on various portions of the body.

Table 1.3). The problem with this approach is that it makes inadequate allowance for variations in muscle mass. For example, the weight of a well-muscled athlete involved in strength and power sports is likely to exceed the ideal weight for his or her height found in an actuarial table. From a purely statistical standpoint, such an individual would be described as overweight, but this may not be a meaningful description. Clearly, there are times when the term overweight can be misleading.

    Obesity, on the other hand, is a more precise term. Defined as an excess of body fat, it can be quantitatively measured by

Obesity: An excessive accumulation of body fat.

(continued on p. 14)

Table 1.3 Metropolitan Life Table of Desirable Body Weight Ranges

	MEN					WOMEN			
Height Feet	Inches	Small Frame	Medium Frame	Large Frame	Height Feet	Inches	Small Frame	Medium Frame	Large Frame
5	2	128–134	131–141	138–150	4	10	102–111	109–121	118–131
5	3	130–136	133–143	140–153	4	11	103–113	111–123	120–134
5	4	132–138	135–145	142–156	5	0	104–115	113–126	122–137
5	5	134–140	137–148	144–160	5	1	106–118	115–129	125–140
5	6	136–142	139–151	146–164	5	2	108–121	118–132	128–143
5	7	138–145	142–154	149–168	5	3	111–124	121–135	131–147
5	8	140–148	145–157	152–172	5	4	114–127	124–138	134–151
5	9	142–151	148–160	155–176	5	5	117–130	127–141	137–155
5	10	144–154	151–163	158–180	5	6	120–133	130–144	140–159
5	11	146–157	154–166	161–184	5	7	123–136	133–147	143–163
6	0	149–160	157–170	164–188	5	8	126–139	136–150	146–167
6	1	152–164	160–174	168–192	5	9	129–142	139–153	149–170
6	2	155–168	164–178	172–197	5	10	132–145	142–156	152–173
6	3	158–172	167–182	176–202	5	11	135–148	145–159	155–176
6	4	162–176	171–187	181–207	6	0	138–151	148–162	158–179

Note: Weights at ages 25–59 based on lowest mortality. Weight in pounds according to frame (in indoor clothing weighing 5 lbs. for men and 3 lbs. for women; shoes with 1″ heels).

The Metropolitan Life Insurance Company tables of desirable weights (copyright 1983, Metropolitan Life Insurance Company) were most recently revised in 1983. To determine your frame size, extend one arm and bend the forearm upward at a 90 degree angle. Keeping your fingers straight, turn the inside of one wrist toward your body. Then place the thumb and index finger of your other hand on the two prominent bones on either side of your bent elbow. Pull your fingers away while maintaining the space between them. Then measure this space and compare it to the numbers in the table to the right. If your measurement falls within the range listed here, you have a medium frame. If it is smaller, you have a small frame. If it is larger, you have a large frame.

MEN	
Height in 1 inch heels	Elbow breadth
5′2″ – 5′3″	2$\frac{1}{2}$″ – 2$\frac{7}{8}$″
5′4″ – 5′7″	2$\frac{5}{8}$″ – 2$\frac{7}{8}$″
5′8″ – 5′11″	2$\frac{3}{4}$″ – 3″
6′0″ – 6′3″	2$\frac{3}{4}$″ – 3$\frac{1}{8}$″
6′4″	2$\frac{7}{8}$″ – 3$\frac{1}{4}$″

WOMEN	
Height in 1 inch heels	Elbow breadth
4′10″ – 4′11″	2$\frac{1}{4}$″ – 2$\frac{1}{2}$″
5′0″ – 5′3″	2$\frac{1}{4}$″ – 2$\frac{1}{2}$″
5′4″ – 5′7″	2$\frac{3}{8}$″ – 2$\frac{5}{8}$″
5′8″ – 5′11″	2$\frac{3}{8}$″ – 2$\frac{5}{8}$″
6′0″	2$\frac{1}{2}$″ – 2$\frac{3}{4}$″

Source: Society of Actuaries, and Association of Life Insurance Medical Directors of America, *1979 Build Study,* 1980.

Table 1.4 Generally Accepted Ranges for Percentage of Body Fat

Classification	Male	Female
Lean	<8%	<13%
Optimal	8–15%	13–20%
Slightly overfat	16–20%	21–25%
Fat	21–24%	26–32%
Obese (overfat)	≥25%	≥32%

Source: Adapted from T. G. Lohman, "The Use of Skinfold to Estimate Body Fatness on Children and Youth," *Journal of Physical Education, Recreation, and Dance* (November/December 1987), pp. 98–102.

The classification of body fat percentages shown here is generally accepted at the present time. It should be emphasized, however, that acceptable body fat percentages vary from individual to individual and that there is some disagreement among experts concerning the validity of any classification scheme—including the one depicted here.

determining the individual's **percentage of body fat**. Opinions vary, however, on just what percentage of body fat constitutes obesity, and exact standards have yet to be developed.

Generally, a woman is considered to be borderline obese at 30 to 35 percent body fat, and obese at more than 35 percent. For men the equivalent numbers are, respectively, 20 to 25 percent and more than 25 percent. [14] Unfortunately, it is as difficult to define an ideal body-fat percentage as it is to define an ideal body weight. [15] The acceptable range of body-fat percentage depends on several factors, including age, sex, and level of physical activity. While some male athletes have been found to have body-fat percentages as low as 4 to 5 percent, a generally agreed-upon healthy range for women aged 20 to 29 is 16 to 30 percent body fat. For men of the same ages, the range is 12 to 25 percent. [16] (See Table 1.3.) The ranges are slightly higher for women than for men, because women have additional deposits of fat on their breasts and hips.

It should be noted here that while obesity is harmful, so too are unrealistically low targets for weight and body-fat percentage. With few exceptions, it is counterproductive and sometimes even dangerous to focus on achieving a particular percentage of body fat. Further, an unrelenting quest to lower one's body-fat percentage to some specific level is very unwise. This is partic-

Percentage of body fat: The percent of total body weight that is composed of fat; the ratio of the weight of *total body fat* to the weight of the *fat-free mass*.

Using Percent of Body Fat to Calculate an Ideal Target Weight

Steve, who currently weights 196 pounds, has recently had the privilege of experiencing a hydrostatic weighing test. Based on the results of that test, he would like to calculate his ideal weight using a desired body fat percentage of 19 percent. The results of Steve's test are as follows:

Age:	26 years
Weight:	196 pounds
Percent of body fat:	23% (average range)
Fat Mass (FM)	196 × 0.23 = 45 pounds
Fat-Free Mass	196 − 45 = 151 pounds
Desired Percent of Body Fat	19% ("good" range)

To calculate an ideal weight based on Steve's desired percent of body fat, we assume a constant fat-free mass and use the following formula:

$$\text{Ideal body weight} = \frac{\text{Fat-free mass}}{(1.00 - \text{desired \% in decimal form})}$$

$$\text{Ideal body weight} = \frac{151 \text{ lbs.}}{1.00 - 0.19} = 186 \text{ pounds}$$

This tells us that if Steve maintains all of his fat-free mass and loses 10 lbs. of fat, he will weigh 186 lbs. and be approximately 19% body fat.

Did You Know That . . .

Exercise is one of the few factors that researchers have found to play a beneficial role in long-term maintenance of body weight.

ularly so when such a quest is a symptom of an underlying eating disorder such as **anorexia nervosa** or **bulimia**, the incidence of which has increased dramatically in recent years. Such disorders are potentially life-threatening, and sufferers should be strongly encouraged to seek medical advice.

As with heart disease—or many other conditions, for that matter—we are better able to define obesity than to explain its causes. It is clear that people who consume more calories than they expend can expect to gain weight. Similarly, it is a relatively simple matter to measure the number of calories consumed. Measuring caloric expenditure, however, is a much more difficult proposition, since it seems to vary considerably from person to person and situation to situation.

Anorexia nervosa: A psychological and physiological condition characterized by a refusal or inability to eat, leading to severe weight loss, malnutrition, hormonal imbalance, and other potentially life-threatening changes.

Bulimia: A psychological and physiological condition characterized by recurrent episodes of binge eating, usually followed by self-induced vomiting, use of laxatives or diuretics, or vigorous exercise in order to prevent weight gain.

As a result, there is at the present time no single generally accepted theory of the causes of obesity. Diet, heredity, life-style, physiological, and even psychological factors all seem to contribute. One of the more important of these factors is the **resting metabolic rate**, which varies significantly from person to person. Measured in calories consumed per unit of time, resting metabolic rate can be defined as the energy cost of maintaining bodily functions. All other things being equal (which they seldom are!), we would expect someone with a relatively low resting metabolic rate to gain weight more easily than someone with a relatively high one. However, differences in resting metabolic rate appear to be but one of a number of factors that may contribute to obesity.

Regardless of what causes obesity, it is clear that, in most instances, exercise is a useful tool for combating it. A sound exercise program contributes to weight management by increasing the body's energy expenditure. Assuming no offsetting increase in food intake, such a program effectively reduces the number of calories available for conversion into storage fat. Given exercise's many other benefits, this is a major plus, and it helps to explain why exercise is a basic component of many professionally designed and monitored weight-control programs. (For a more detailed discussion of obesity and weight control, see the volume in this series entitled *Wellness: Weight Control* by Randall R. Cottrell.)

MAKING EXERCISE A PART OF YOUR LIFE

Public awareness of health and other quality-of-life issues has increased dramatically in recent years. Today, it is virtually impossible to read a newspaper or magazine or listen to a radio or television news program without coming across a health-related feature or item. The quality of such reports is sometimes less than excellent. Nevertheless, they have helped us realize that we all need to make a conscious and sustained effort to improve or maintain our good health.

The current interest in wellness arises, to a large extent, from an attempt to identify and encourage alternatives to the sedentary way of life. Exercise, along with good nutrition, adequate sleep, and other wise behaviors is coming to be widely recognized as a critical component of a healthier life-style.

The health benefits of regular exercise have been confirmed by numerous research studies. Certainly, exercise should not be viewed as a cure for all physical ailments. However, its integra-

Resting metabolic rate: The rate of energy consumption necessary to maintain the body and perform vital body functions (breathing, heartbeat, maintenance of body temperature, etc.) at rest; increases in activity level result in corresponding increases in the metabolic rate.

(continued on p. 21)

It's Easy to Get Fit

The benefits of exercise are old news to this nation of self-avowed couch potatoes, but health experts supply convincing evidence that we should—indeed, must—acquire a love of physical fitness. If you're someone who groans at the suggestion of sweat, you'll be happy to discover that you don't have to exercise much to reap the benefits. But you will have a lot to lose if you don't exercise at all.

Those who don't work out because they "feel fine" aren't taking into consideration the mounting evidence linking life-threatening illnesses with inactivity. "There is a strong tendency to think of many major diseases, such as heart disease, hypertension, and diabetes, as being elderly or middle-aged problems," comments cardiologist James M. Rippe, director of the Exercise Physiology Laboratory at the University of Massachusetts Medical School, in Worcester, "but in fact, the roots of these diseases are in childhood." The more sedentary the parent is, the more likely the child will be as well. Not surprisingly, doctors have found evidence of deterioration of the heart and arteries in persons as young as twenty years of age.

Although most of the research into the relationship between heart disease and lifestyle has focused on men, physicians are discovering that women have almost as many heart attacks as men and have far graver prospects for recovery. According to a study of more than 2,800 healthy women, those who don't exercise are three times more likely to die prematurely from a heart attack than are women who do work out.

It's certainly easy to adapt to a sedentary lifestyle; elevators are faster than stairs, a drive in a warm car is more comfortable than a walk in chilly weather. But these convenient time-savers nearly eliminate the need for physical exertion.

As the extra pounds add up from lack of activity, our risk increases for such serious illnesses as adult-onset diabetes, respiratory problems, and high blood pressure. In addition to controlling weight gain, exercise helps protect against osteoporosis, acts as a natural tranquilizer, and may even play a part in preventing certain types of cancer.

Getting physical.

The body responds almost immediately to exercise, quickly making adjustments to accommodate the increased physical demands. Barbara L. Drinkwater, Ph.D., president of the American College of Sports Medicine, explains, "The body is a constantly renewable resource, and if you ask for more, it will eventually be able to give you more. No matter how old you are, if you start becoming active, your body will improve its functional capacity. Even women in their eighties have benefited from beginning an exercise program."

There's no getting around the fact that exercise sometimes feels uncomfortable. The prospect of sweating, breathing heavily, and having your heart pound is hardly an incentive to start an exercise program, and aching muscles may make you think twice about returning the next day for more. It may help to know that these responses are positive signs that your body is working hard to help make exercise easier for you.

The muscles need oxygen to perform, and they depend on the body's most important muscle—the heart—to transport it to them. During exercise the heart works harder to circulate the blood, which carries the oxygen, throughout the body. Far from breaking the body down, the increased demands of exercise stimulate it to work more efficiently. It's the inactive heart that weakens, compensating for its lack of strength by beating more frequently to circulate the blood. A strong heart can circulate more blood per beat, using its power to successfully meet the muscles' demands for oxygen.

Exercise enthusiasts know from experience that the stiffness and soreness following an exercise session are signals that the muscles are out of shape, but the aches quickly subside once physical activity becomes routine. Like the heart, the muscular system responds positively to exercise. Anaerobic (literally, without oxygen) exercise produces the most dramatic results. Activities like weight lifting and sprinting pump up the muscles, increasing the number of muscle fibers. These exercises build strength but do little to improve one's cardiovascular capacity unless combined with aerobic exercises, such as running, swimming, or dancing. These activities require oxygen for energy as well as the glucose and fatty acids stored in the body. Regular exercise improves the body's capacity to conserve and use these fuels, allowing for longer workouts that feel less strenuous.

A body that can handle a vigorous workout can better manage the demands of day-to-day living. Flexibility, agility, and better coordination are also some of the bonuses of regular exercise, which is why active people tend to be less accident-prone and report feeling better about their bodies, more in control. For these reasons, Drinkwater chooses to define being fit as being able to "meet the challenges of everyday living with energy on reserve."

Reaping the benefits.

Of course, having some extra energy is always appealing, but losing weight is most often the real motive behind starting an exercise program. But can exercise alone get rid of extra pounds? The answer is a qualified yes. Exercise has a direct effect on the metabolism, raising it for a few hours following a workout. But according to the American College of Sports Medicine, if you want to lose weight simply by exercising, without restricting your food intake, you're going to have to exercise at least four days a week for a minimum of 50 minutes. You can lose the weight as effectively if you combine exercise with a modest decrease, about 500 to 1,000 calories a day, in your calorie consumption.

Losing weight is one of the reasons exercise feels good inside and out. It also improves your self-image and serves as a physical release of inner tensions and frustrations. Scientifically speaking, exercise fuels the production of "stress busters," chemicals the body releases to promote relaxation. In fact, exercise has been clini-

cally proven to alleviate mild depression and can also act as a natural antidote to insomnia.

Some fitness experts say that for you to enjoy these benefits, exercise need not be more strenuous than a daily stint in the garden, weeding and digging—the point being that it is enough to be *active* and that the intensity of your workout is less important. But many scientists who have examined the relationship between exercise and disease prevention don't agree. So far, the American College of Sports Medicine has not felt it necessary to reduce their recommendations for effective fitness conditioning. They suggest that a person exercise aerobically three to five days a week, for between 15 and 60 minutes, reaching at least 60 percent of his or her maximum heart rate (pulse beats per minute). To calculate your maximum heart rate, subtract your age from 220.

Fitness experts do recognize that Americans can't necessarily relate to these abstract guidelines. "People have erected barriers for themselves by thinking that if they don't exercise a certain way, then they shouldn't bother at all," observes Rippe, "but in order to exercise optimally for your health, you should concentrate on consistency, not intensity."

To help people incorporate more physical activity into their day, researchers are turning their attention toward finding better motivation techniques and simpler exercise routines. According to Susan Johnson, Ed.D., director of continuing education at the Institute for Aerobics Research in Dallas, first-time exercisers need positive reinforcement from a fitness regimen that isn't too difficult. She recommends working out with a partner, preferably your spouse so that you won't lose time with your family. She also suggests alternating different types of low-impact exercises to break the monotony, switching off cycling and walking, for instance. What probably won't help, Johnson cautions, is spending a lot of money before you establish an exercise routine, either on equipment or health-club memberships, hoping the expense will pressure you to stick with it. "I can't tell you how many people have bought exercise equipment and now it's just sitting in their basements," she says.

EXERCISING YOUR OPTIONS

	Why it's good	The drawbacks	Keep in mind
WALKING	Convenient; fun to do with a friend; low injury potential; good cardiovascular conditioner.	None.	Simple to work into your daily routine; must walk energetically to boost heart rate.
JOGGING	Good aerobic conditioner for all ages.	Neglecting to warm up properly could lead to injuries.	Beginners should start with a slow jog to build up their stamina.
SWIMMING	Good conditioner for the whole body; support of water protects muscles and joints from injury.	Must be a competent swimmer to reap fitness benefits; need access to pool.	Research has shown that swimming does not promote weight loss.
CYCLING	Good cardiovascular conditioner; easy on the joints.	Requires good weather or access to a stationary bike.	Sophisticated new cycling machines change resistance level to imitate cycling outdoors.
ROWING	Works out heart and lungs; strengthens arms, legs, stomach, and back.	Rowing machines can be expensive.	May be a good investment once you've established a regular routine.
JUMPING ROPE	Good rainy-day aerobic conditioner.	Can be tedious.	Keep your jumps low to minimize stress on joints.
AEROBIC DANCING	If the routine is safe and well choreographed, an excellent cardiovascular and muscular workout.	Requires health-club or dance-studio membership; bad instruction can be hazardous.	Make sure instructors are certified; observe a class to see if there is individual guidance offered.
TENNIS	A good game of singles tennis burns as many calories as a brisk walk.	Must be a skilled player to achieve a vigorous aerobic workout.	Improves your hand-eye coordination.
GOLF	A favorite for relaxation; walking the course can be invigorating.	Contributes little to improving fitness levels.	Good opportunity to get outdoors.
SOFTBALL	Fun social activity; good opportunity to play with your kids.	Lots of stopping and starting, so there is little aerobic benefit.	Consider this a complement to your regular fitness routine.

A walk around the block.

Fortunately, the latest exercise craze is one that delights fitness experts and amateur athletes alike. Recent research concerning the cardiovascular benefits of walking have shown surprisingly positive results. Doctors asked 300 healthy men and women to walk merely one mile briskly and found that for 67 percent of the men and 91 percent of the women, this simple, convenient form of exercise stimulated the heart to reach a rate considered optimal for cardiovascular improvement.

A brisk walk, it should be noted, is not the same as a leisurely stroll. Walking for exercise must engage the whole body, arms swinging and legs striding at a quick pace. "Walking should not leave you breathless," advises Johnson, "but the effort should make you breathe deeply, as when you are hurrying to make a late appointment."

Could walking be the perfect solution for even the most adamant couch potato? Doctors hope so, pointing out how little time a brisk walk takes and the low injury potential of striding through your neighborhood or the local mall in sneakers. Unfortunately, there will always be the disgruntled faction of Americans who adamantly refuse to exercise, but don't let them discourage you. If spending just an hour a day on yourself will increase your active healthy hours on Earth, the effort is certainly well worth it.

Source: Alix Finkelstein, *Parents* (July 1989), pp. 170–175.

FIGURE 1.5
Mortality Rates and Fitness

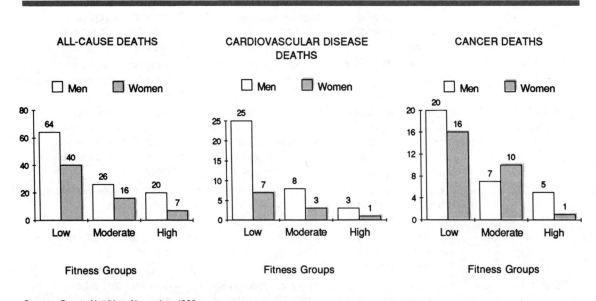

Source: *Sports Nutrition*, November 1990.

According to a recent study, lack of exercise and low levels of physical fitness are significant risk factors for disease and early death. As the graphs shown here demonstrate, increases in fitness lead to a striking decline in death rates for both men and women.

tion into daily life is a positive step toward improved health that all of us can make.

Some obstacles stand in the way of incorporating exercise into our daily routines. Those of us wishing to do so are in for a challenge. One of the most common problems is lack of time. Learning to set aside hours for exercise on a regular basis can be difficult. Another major impediment is the sheer volume of information regarding exercise programs that is currently available. Much of it is contradictory or confusing—even wrong. Trying to choose the right information and guidance can be a daunting task.

The biggest obstacle, however, is probably psychological. Even if time and the right information are readily available, making the commitment to exercise on a regular basis—as a way of life—requires strong motivation, effort, and discipline.

Notwithstanding these and other obstacles, you can find ample guidance, opportunity, and encouragement to meet your exercise goals. What is more, it is likely that the most rapid and apparent benefits, such as increased strength and endurance, will soon reinforce your motivation and enthusiasm. And eventually you may find that your *need* to exercise has been transformed into the *desire* to exercise.

Did You Know That . . .

Because fats leave the stomach slowly, avoid consuming fat just before exercising.

Exercise, Fitness, and Training

WE HEAR SUCH TERMS as "physically fit" or "physical fitness" every day. Most of us use the word **fitness** to refer to a feeling and appearance of good health. But what does it really mean? In truth, fitness is an elusive term that defies easy description. In fact, there is no single definition of fitness. Rather, fitness may be defined in a variety of ways, and any discussion of fitness must begin with an explanation of the way in which the user intends to define the term.

THE CONCEPT OF FITNESS

The American College of Sports Medicine (ACSM) notes, "The term 'health-related physical fitness' has been used to denote fitness as it pertains to disease prevention and health promotion." Fitness is, according to ACSM, "A state characterized by (a) an ability to perform daily activities with vigor, and (b) demonstration of traits and capacities that are associated with low risk of premature development of the hypokinetic diseases (i.e., those associated with physical inactivity)." [1]

Fitness is sometimes also described in quantitative terms using measures such as heart rate, endurance, blood pressure, or blood cholesterol level. These valuable measures may be indicative of one's general state of health and thus are certainly related to fitness.

The Components of Fitness
Yet another way of discussing fitness – and it is the approach that we follow in this book – is to divide it into five basic components.

Fitness: The ability to meet the demands of daily living with energy to spare; possessing the functional capacity to do not only those tasks that are required, but also those activities that one enjoys.

If you want to be sedentary, that's your business, right? Certainly, if you want to pass up the potential benefits provided by being physically active, that affects only you. But now a study by the RAND Corporation, published in a recent issue of the *American Journal of Public Health,* shows that an individual's sedentary habits impose a price on other members of society—to the tune of a $1,900 lifetime subsidy.

The High Cost of Doing Nothing

This figure includes various "external costs"—costs others pay as a result of a person's decision to lead a comparatively inactive life rather than exercise—such as additional medical costs, increased health-insurance payments, sick-leave pay, disability insurance, and losses in job productivity. The total would be considerably more than $1,900 if not for the offsetting fact that sedentary individuals tend to die earlier and therefore collect less in pensions and Social Security. The researchers tried to take into account the possibility that some people who exercise a lot may be healthier than average to begin with.

The societal costs of smoking and drinking are offset, at least in part, by excise taxes paid on cigarettes and alcoholic beverages. But, as the RAND researchers point out, we can't tax a sedentary life-style. They suggest that subsidies to programs (such as corporate wellness activities) and recreational facilities (such as public parks) that encourage exercise will save us money in the long run.

We've discussed the benefits of exercise from many angles, but maybe this new approach will make some converts.

Source: *University of California Berkeley Wellness Letter,* December 1989, p. 3.

These are **cardiovascular fitness, muscular strength, muscular endurance, flexibility,** and **body composition**.

- Cardiovascular fitness is the ability of the heart, lungs, and blood vessels to supply fuel, especially oxygen, to the muscles during continuous activity [2], and the ability of the muscles to take up and utilize what is delivered. This is also known as *aerobic fitness.*
- Muscular strength refers to the ability of a muscle or group of muscles to exert force.
- Muscular endurance is the ability of a muscle or group of muscles to sustain a particular level of force.
- Flexibility is the range of motion available at a joint or combination of joints.

Cardiovascular fitness: The ability of the heart and blood vessels to supply fuel, especially oxygen, to the muscles during continuous activity, and the ability of the muscles to take up and utilize the oxygen that is delivered. Also called aerobic fitness.

Muscular strength: The ability of a muscle or group of muscles to exert a maximal amount of force.

Muscular endurance: The ability of a muscle or group of muscles to sustain a given level of force.

Flexibility: The range of motion available at a joint or combination of joints.

Body composition: The relative percentages of fat and fat-free mass.

• Body composition refers to the relative percentages of fat and fat-free mass (as discussed in chapter 1).

The goals of an exercise program will vary from individual to individual. Athletes, for example, usually view exercise as a means of enhancing their athletic performance. The rest of us, however, are more likely to be interested in exercise as a means of improving or maintaining our general health and fitness. The ability of any exercise program to help us accomplish these goals depends first and foremost on consistency. It is not enough merely to exercise every now and then. Most of the benefits of exercise are cumulative. Thus, only an exercise program that involves regular and sufficient amounts of exercise will help us realize our objective.

The proper approach to starting an exercise program is to determine and set realistic fitness goals, find an activity or activities well-suited to help us meet those goals and to our personal needs or interests, and then pursue those goals conscientiously and sensibly. Participation in a well-structured exercise program enables mere exercise to become **training**.

Training: A program of regular exercise of a frequency, intensity, and duration sufficient to produce a measurable improvement in one or more fitness components.

VO₂ max: The maximum quantity of oxygen that can be delivered to and consumed by the organs of the body at any given time; also known as maximum oxygen uptake, VO_2 max is usually measured as either liters of oxygen (O_2) consumed per minute (absolute VO_2 max) or as liters of oxygen consumed per minute divided by body weight in kilograms (relative VO_2 max).

Energy Use During Exercise

The metabolic process by which the body supplies itself with energy is called cellular respiration. It is broken down into two phases: the anaerobic and the aerobic.

Extremely high intensity exercise of short duration (from seconds to a few minutes) draws primarily on the body's anaerobic sources of energy. Such activity requires more energy than the body can supply from aerobic sources, even when heart rate and blood flow, and the muscles' supply of oxygen, is at their maximum. In other words, the **VO₂ max** (the maximum amount of oxygen the cardiovascular system can supply to body tissue) has been exceeded. Under these conditions, energy must be obtained directly from the muscle cells rather than from stores of fat and carbohydrates. The process of deriving energy from the muscle cells without oxygen supplied by the cardiovascular system is called anaerobic respiration.

Aerobic respiration uses oxygen to chemically convert fat and carbohydrate stores into energy. In endurance exercises such as long distance running or cycling, energy is supplied by aerobic respiration. Because the intensity is below the body's VO₂ max, and because the exercise lasts relatively long (minutes to hours), the circulatory system has time to deliver the oxygen necessary for this process to take place.

When you think of oxygen consumption during aerobic exercise, you may think of an untrained runner huffing and puffing around a track while practiced runners glide past, maybe even carrying on a conversation. The untrained runner's heart rate has skyrocketed, while the trained runner's heart rate is moderate. Is this because a practiced runner does not require as much oxygen for aerobic respiration as an untrained runner? In fact, the amount of oxygen necessary to fuel the body while running a mile is the same in both trained and untrained persons of the same height and weight. Thus, the amount of oxygen that is delivered to their organs must also be the same. What happens in a physically fit individual is that through aerobic exercise the heart muscle gets stronger and is therefore able to pump more blood—carrying more oxygen—per beat, known as an increased *stroke volume*. Indeed, it is not uncommon for stroke volume to increase by 30 to 50 percent as a result of endurance or aerobic training. Anaerobic exercise will increase muscle strength, but has no particular benefits for the cardiovascular system.

Did You Know That . . .

Every day of inactivity will require two days of activity to get back to the level of fitness achieved earlier.

THE CONCEPT OF TRAINING

Measurable improvement in any of the 5 fitness components requires a regular, systematic program of exercises that are appropriate to one's specific objectives. A single bout of weight lifting, for example, is unlikely to bring about significant improvements in muscular strength. That is because one bout of exercise is not training. In its truest sense, training is a regular program of exercise of a frequency, intensity, and duration sufficient to bring about measurable physiological changes. This adaptation is known as the **training effect.**

Training must be specifically designed to the type of fitness desired. It is important to note that the form and extent of the training effect resulting from each type of training will vary from person to person and from activity to activity.

While women and men differ in basic body composition, training does not appear to affect women any differently than men. It is true, however, that younger persons generally respond more readily to training, realizing larger percentage improvements in their conditioning from the same amount of training than older people. However, this is not to say that older people do not benefit from exercise. On the contrary, a well-designed exercise program will significantly improve conditioning at any age.

Training effect: Measurable physiological changes resulting from a program of regular exercise incorporating appropriate frequency, intensity, and duration for the individual's needs.

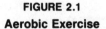

FIGURE 2.1
Aerobic Exercise

Aerobic exercise such as running or jogging stimulates the cardiorespiratory system by increasing the heart rate and the volume of blood pumped by the heart, as well as increasing the consumption of oxygen.

Further, studies have shown that some older adults will show improvement rivaling that of much younger individuals.

Essentially, then, training is exercise with a purpose. Without the appearance of a training effect, there is no real improvement in physical fitness.

But, you might ask, can a relatively modest exercise program that does not produce a training effect nonetheless improve physical health? In other words, can one derive health benefits from exercise even in the absence of measurable improvements in one or more of the 5 fitness components? This is a question on which experts currently disagree. For the moment then, perhaps

(continued on p. 28)

Making the Heart Stronger

In terms of longevity, a little exercise goes a long way—and more exercise may go even further. Such are the encouraging conclusions of two recent studies. One, the largest ever to measure the effects of fitness on longevity, showed that you needn't be a marathon runner to reap the benefits of exercise. Subjects were divided into five groups according to fitness levels. As expected, the least fit were most likely to die first, and death rates—from cancer as well as from cardiovascular problems—were lowest in the most fit. However, the greatest leap in longevity was found in those who shifted from sedentary habits to engaging in low levels of exercise (such as brisk walking for 30 minutes three or four days a week).

The other study, presented at the annual meeting of the American Heart Association, showed that exercise has benefits above and beyond the introductory level, and may even be an anti-aging treatment of sorts. It found that strenuous exercise improved the body's ability to break down life-threatening blood clots by increasing levels of the clot-dissolving protein TPA (tissue plasminogen activator). TPA, which is produced naturally by cells in the blood vessels, can also be manufactured in the laboratory and . . . can lessen damage to the heart muscle when administered quickly following a heart attack. But if natural levels of TPA are high—as they tend to be in younger people—or can be boosted, they may help to prevent a heart attack in the first place.

In this study, done at two Seattle medical centers, researchers found that strenuous exercise by older men (average age 65) led to a 40% average increase in resting levels of TPA, and a significant drop in levels of the clot-building protein fibrinogen. The subjects did 45 minutes of aerobic exercise a day, four to five days a week. (N.B.: Subjects were thoroughly evaluated and found healthy at the start of this program. You should get an okay from your doctor before you embark on any exercise program, especially a strenuous one.)

"After six months, the older exercisers' fibrinolytic (clot-busting) systems were comparable to those of healthy younger persons," says Dr. Wayne Chandler, one of the researchers. He notes that the researchers can only assume that there will be a decrease in the incidence of heart attack as a result of these increases in TPA; more extensive, long-term studies are needed to prove that this reduction does, in fact, occur. Together, though, the studies reinforce the same point: Make exercise a part of your life and you might live longer.

Source: *The Johns Hopkins Medical Letter, Health After 50*, Vol. 1, No. 12, February 1990, p. 1.

Did You Know That . . .

In 1772, Dr. Benjamin Rush published *Sermons to Gentlemen Upon Temperance and Exercise*, one of the first fitness manuals in North America.

the best available answer is the following statement from the American College of Sports Medicine: "The health value of regular exercise is confirmed by numerous research studies, and broad recommendations to the public to be physically active are appropriate." [3]

Training for Cardiovascular Fitness

Training to achieve cardiovascular, or **aerobic**, fitness consists of activities that exercise large muscle groups (the leg and arm muscles, for example), that can be maintained for prolonged periods, and that are rhythmic in nature. Distance running, biking, swimming, walking, hiking, jogging, cross-country skiing, dancing, rowing, skipping rope, climbing stairs, skating, and various games that involve endurance will all improve aerobic fitness.

The purpose of aerobic training is to promote changes in various aspects of the **cardiovascular system** as well as muscular endurance. Aerobic exercises stimulate the cardiovascular system and cause the heart to increase its pumping volume, thereby increasing the delivery of blood and oxygen to the muscles.

Aerobic training also produces marked changes in other parts of the body. An increased number of capillaries (the smallest blood vessels in the body) will appear in the major skeletal muscles involved (the leg muscles in runners, for example, or the leg and arm muscles in cross-country skiers). Perhaps in part because of this increase in the number of capillaries, these muscles will show an increased ability to consume oxygen and will increase their use of fat as an energy source while reducing their use of carbohydrates. The result is an increase in the ability of these muscles to sustain long-term activity (endurance). [4] However, these changes will be confined to the active muscles involved. Further, aerobic training does not enlarge muscles or increase muscular strength. That is the job of strength training.

Training for Muscular Strength

Strength is the ability of a muscle or muscle group to generate force. [5] It is often measured as the amount of force that can be delivered when the muscle is maximally contracting voluntarily. The basic principle involved in strength training is that the exercising muscle must contract against a significant resistance in order to increase its size and consequently its strength. Just as in aerobic training, realization of a training effect in strength

Aerobic: Having to do with oxygen. Aerobic exercise is exercise designed to produce a sustained increase in heart rate and whose energy costs can be met by the body from aerobic sources, i.e., from increased oxygen consumption.

Cardiovascular system: The heart and blood vessels; the circulatory system.

training requires adequate frequency, intensity, and duration of exercise.

The weight loads used to train for muscular strength are often expressed as a percentage of a person's **one repetition maximum (1RM)**, which is the maximum weight a person can move through the range of motion for one repetition of a particular exercise. The value of 1RM will vary from exercise to exercise and individual to individual. If the maximum weight you can bench press is 100 pounds, then 100 pounds is your 1RM value for this particular exercise. Someone else's 1RM value for this exercise may be much larger or smaller. Similarly, it is unlikely your 1RM value for a different exercise, the leg press, for example, will also be 100 pounds.

Training loads greater than or equal to 75 percent of a person's 1RM with 3 or more sets of 5 to 10 repetitions each are often considered optimal for increasing muscular strength. [6] However, training loads of less than 75 percent of a person's 1RM can also be effective, especially with previously untrained individuals.

At the beginning of a program, weight training should be performed 2 to 3 times per week. Later, the frequency can be increased as appropriate, based on the individual's response to the program.

The three basic types of muscular strength training correspond to the three basic types of muscular contractions, which are normally performed against a source of resistance: isometric, isotonic (sometimes called "dynamic"), and isokinetic.

In **isometric exercise**, the force is applied against an immovable object (such as a wall or heavy weight), and thus there is little or no change in the length of the muscle. In **isotonic exercise**, the force overcomes the resistance and the muscle moves, changing its length in the process. **Isokinetic exercise** involves moving a limb at constant velocity. However, it is difficult to achieve "pure" isokinetic movement in practice, so these exercises often are really isotonic.

Isometric Exercise Isometric training programs involving as few as 5 contractions, 3 times per week, have been shown to be moderately effective in building strength in specific muscles. [7] Isometric contractions also occur during isotonic exercise at what is commonly called the **sticking point**, the point at which the weight being used exceeds that which the muscle is capable of moving.

Although isometric exercise can produce increases in

One repetition maximum (1RM): The maximum weight a person can move through the range of motion for one repetition of a particular exercise.

Isometric exercise: Strength training involving the application of force against an immovable object (such as a wall or heavy weight); in isometric exercise there is little or no change in the length of the muscle.

Isotonic exercise: Strength training involving a fixed resistance that can be overcome by the muscle, resulting in the movement of the muscle and changes in its length; also called dynamic exercise.

Isokinetic exercise: Strength training in which there is an attempt to move the joint or limb involved at a constant velocity.

Sticking point: The point at which the weight being moved is greater than the muscle's ability to move it.

FIGURE 2.2
Muscular Strength Training

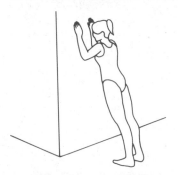

Isometric
Isometric exercise involves muscle groups exerting pressure against an immovable object, such as a wall. There is little change in the length of the muscles used.

Isotonic
Isotonic exercise uses force to overcome resistance. The muscles exerting pressure will move and lengthen. Free weights, variable resistance machines, and a person's own body can be used to create the resistance.

Isokinetic
Isokinetic exercise requires special equipment to move reasonably heavy weights at a constant speed. Specific muscles are exercised and put through their full range of movement.

The three basic types of muscular strength training correspond to the three basic types of muscular contractions: isometric, isotonic, and isokinetic.

strength, this form of training, once quite popular, has fallen out of favor. It is ineffective for producing large strength increases, and those increases in strength that do occur are often limited to a very narrow range of movement, namely the joint angle at which the exercise is performed. Another drawback is the lack of means to monitor progress. Isometric training may also cause undesirable increases in blood pressure, which is of particular concern to older adults and those with hypertension.

Isotonic Exercise   Isotonic-type training is the most popular and versatile method of increasing strength. It has four subtypes: constant load (free weights and some machines), variable resistance (Nautilus-type machines); plyometric; and speed resistance training. [8]

Constant load isotonic training involves movements wherein the resistance is constant, such as with barbells, dumbbells, and some weight machines. In each exercise, the joint angle changes as a person's limb moves the weight through a certain range of motion. As the joint angle changes, so does the force that the muscle must use to move the weight. The maximum amount of weight that can be used here is limited by the angle at which the muscle's effective force is at its lowest value.

Variable resistance (also known as dynamic accommodating resistance, or DAR) exercises are performed on machines that are designed to change (vary) the resistance automatically throughout the exercise in response to the varying levels of force exerted by the exercising muscles at different joint angles. This is accomplished by means of machines utilizing a kidney-shaped cam (or, in some machines, a sleeve-like device). By better matching resistance force to muscle force throughout the entire range of motion, this type of equipment reduces the risk of injury while offering enhanced strength-building potential. Nautilus, some new models of Universal, and similar machines utilize this concept. [9]

Plyometric and *speed resistance* training are often used in an attempt to increase explosive power. Plyometric training employs jumping, hopping, skipping, and other movements that start with a sudden stretch of the active muscle followed by a voluntary contraction of the stretching muscles. This type of training is most often used in preparation for activities that involve jumping and rapid changes of direction, because the training directly mimics the activity. Speed resistance training consists of attempts to move weights as rapidly and explosively as possible (as in Olympic weight lifting). While popular among Olympic weight lifters and other seriously competitive athletes, its effectiveness has not been well documented.

The risks of plyometric and speed resistance training lie in the ballistic style of movement involved. Strains, tears, and other damage to muscles, joints, and connective tissue are possible, particularly in the absence of complete instruction and thorough warm-up. Athletes in several sports use these techniques with a great deal of success. However, some experts feel that, given the risks cited above, they should be used only by highly trained competitive athletes with healthy musculoskeletal systems.

Isokinetic Exercise Isokinetic training involves the use of machines that attempt to exercise muscles at a constant speed of movement. In this type of training, there are 2 complementary phases to each movement. First, a specific muscle is exercised through its full range of motion. This is followed by a movement

---

Did You Know That . . .

By age 40 or 50, most people will develop osteoarthritis, a deterioration of the joints in which the bone ends begin to fray and the cartilage that cushions the joints diminishes.

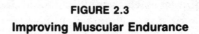

FIGURE 2.3
Improving Muscular Endurance

Aerobic exercise such as swimming can improve muscular endurance—the ability of muscles to sustain long-term activity.

involving the contraction of the **antagonistic muscle** (the one that contracts in the opposite direction in the same range of motion). Isokinetic training is very popular among specialists in physical therapy and rehabilitation.

Generally speaking, strength training results in an increase in muscle size and the capacity of a muscle to develop force. [10] Nevertheless, most strength-training programs will not improve oxygen consumption, as aerobic training does.

Training for Muscular Endurance

Weight training can be used to improve muscular endurance. In contrast to exercises designed mainly for increases in strength, improvement of endurance is best realized by using weights of less than 50 percent of a person's one repetition maximum in multiple sets, with a higher number of repetitions (more than 20). However, it should be noted that the increases in muscle strength brought about by heavy resistance (strength) training will also lead to improvements in muscle endurance.

Muscular endurance exercises routinely include the use of body resistance exercises such as situps or pushups or with

Antagonistic muscle: The muscle that produces the opposite joint action to that of the prime mover or active muscle.

implements such as surgical tubing or light weights. Abdominal curls and lateral raises with dumbbells are examples of such exercises.

For the purpose of a general fitness program, muscular strength and endurance exist on a continuum. Training for both should be incorporated in order to realize the selective benefits of each form. Too much or too little of one can impede the progress of training in the other.

Training for Flexibility

Flexibility is a measure of the range of motion of a joint or group of joints. Although lack of flexibility is seldom a big concern for younger, more active people, flexibility decreases with age and lack of activity. This decrease may severely restrict an older person's ability to perform even the simplest tasks, such as stepping over or reaching up for things or even putting on clothes. Limited flexibility is also associated with lower-back pain and joint problems. Regular activity can increase flexibility. [11] A regular program of stretching is an effective way to avoid the problems encountered when flexibility decreases.

There are several types of flexibility training: static stretching, ballistic stretching, and proprioceptive neuromuscular facilitation (PNF). Each of these methods has potential benefits as well as drawbacks.

Static Stretching   Static stretching is the most common and simplest method of stretching. It is accomplished by slowly moving into the stretched position, then holding the body part to be stretched motionless for 10 to 30 seconds. As flexibility increases, the stretching time and repetitions (3 to 5) of each exercise may increase. Static flexibility training is useful in promoting flexibility, but it does not produce any training effect on the other four fitness components.

Ballistic Stretching   Ballistic stretching uses a bouncing stretch technique, whereby the overload that creates the stretch is provided by the swinging or jerking of the appropriate body segment. An example of this technique is the bouncing stretch that many people use when touching their toes. In this exercise, the upper body is extended farther and farther downward toward the toes, creating a stretch in the back and hamstring muscles.

This method was quite popular during the 1950s and 1960s, but it has since fallen out of favor. Its risk is that sudden jerking movements often cause a muscle to contract and resist the

Did You Know That . . .

Most people can leap about 24 inches. However, Spud Webb, a basketball player with the Atlanta Hawks, can jump 42 inches, about 6 inches shy of the world record.

FIGURE 2.4
Static Stretching

Static stretching is the simplest and safest method for increasing flexibility. It is accomplished by slowly moving into a stretched position and holding the body motionless for 10 to 30 seconds.

stretch. This is associated with a protective reflex mechanism called the stretch reflex, which is stimulated by sudden, jerking movements. The reflex contraction makes the muscle less able to stretch and more prone to injury. Although programs using the ballistic technique have demonstrated improvements in flexibility, the increased risk of muscle injury may outweigh the benefits.

PNF Methods　Recently, PNF-type flexibility training has become popular. This technique has been adapted for use with athletes from the proprioceptive neuromuscular facilitation method commonly used in physical therapy. This is an assisted stretching technique wherein the subject contracts the muscle in direct opposition to an assistant's applied resistance. After 6 to 8 seconds, the contraction is discontinued, and that portion of the body is stretched with the aid of the assistant. The stretch is held for 10 to 30 seconds. The whole sequence is repeated 3 to 6 times. This technique has been shown to be highly effective in producing improvements in flexibility. [12] The drawback is that it is time-consuming and requires a trained assistant.

Training to Alter Body Composition

Many people who take up an exercise program do so out of a desire to change their body composition—to reduce their percentage of body fat or increase their muscle mass or both. Different types of exercise activity have different effects on body composition. In general, cardiovascular or aerobic exercises such as running, biking, and cross-country skiing are thought to be better for helping remove excess body fat because of their relatively high calorie consumption. Resistance or strength exercises, on the other hand, are generally thought to be better for increasing muscle mass. [13]

With regular exercise, body composition will change to a form more suitable for the energy needs of that exercise. This, in turn, will make it easier to perform the activity.

The examples of running and weight lifting, two extremes, will help to illustrate this point. The long-duration aerobic training used by runners tends to produce a relatively light body that has a high percentage of fat-free mass and a very low percentage of body fat. In contrast, competitive weight lifters (not to be confused with body builders) are likely to develop significant muscle mass, but their percentage of body fat may not be as low as that of runners.

It should be noted here, however, that the precise effects of a particular training program on a given individual are heavily influenced by genetics. That is, it is highly unlikely that some individuals will ever be considered "lean and light," even after years of aerobic training. Likewise, even extensive weight training will not turn someone with a very small frame into a heavyweight Olympic weight lifter. In short, training, no matter how extensive, can and will modify body composition, but only within certain limits established by genetic and other factors.

A PROPER APPROACH TO TRAINING

It is essential that any training program be designed with a specific set of goals in mind. A training program designed to

(continued on p. 38)

Did You Know That . . .

An estimated 85 percent of Americans experience low back pain at some time in their adult lives. Next to upper respiratory infections, it's the most common reason people see a physician.

How to Take a Walk

Walking is a safe, simple way to exercise. You're not likely to get injured, and all you need is a good pair of shoes. Your walking shoes should have a roomy toe box, flexible soles with good traction, and a stiff heel cup for stability. Leather soles are too hard, stiff, and slippery. Running shoes, on the other hand, have too much padding, which can make your feet wobble.

Before you begin a walking program, find out how fit you are now by taking the one-mile walking test designed by the Institute for Aerobics Research. First find a track or flat course where you can measure a mile using your car's odometer. Warm up for several minutes by stretching or walking briskly.

Time yourself as you walk the mile as fast as you can without signs of exhaustion, such as dizziness, nausea, or shortness of breath. When you finish, record your heart rate. (Take your pulse for 15 seconds; multiply by four.) Cool down by walking slowly for a few minutes.

Check the table (page 37) to compare your current fitness level to "moderate" fitness. If you walked the mile in less than the range shown for that heart rate, your fitness level is high; if it took you longer than that range, your fitness is low.

A walk on the mild side

. . . Any level of walking can benefit your health. Naturally, the dividends increase as you walk faster, farther, or more often. For previously sedentary people who scored moderate or below on the one-mile walking test, the table below lays out a graduated program of light walking that doesn't require vigorous effort.

The program, suggested by John J. Duncan, Ph.D., of the Institute for Aerobics Research, won't offer optimal cardiopulmonary fitness. But it will moderately improve your fitness level and, the recent research suggests, decrease your risk of cardiovascular disease and early death.

If you begin the walking program and it seems too easy, skip to the next week of the program. Of, if you're already exercising, begin at whatever level is closest to what you're accustomed to doing.

If you want a higher level of cardiopulmonary fitness than that program offers, let your pulse be

(continued on p. 38)

	WALKING PROGRAM			
Week	Distance (miles)	Pace[1] (minutes per mile)	Total time (minutes per walk)	Frequency (days per week)
1	0.5	23	11½	3
2	1.0	23	23	3
3	1.5	23	34½	3
4	1.5	22	33	4
5	2.0	22	44	4
6	2.0	21	42	4
7	2.5	21	52½	4
8	2.5	20	50	4
9	2.5	20	50	4–5
10	3.0	20	60	4–5
11	3.0	19	57	4–5
12	3.0	18	54	4–5

[1]Your approximate walking speed by the end of the week.

ONE-MILE WALKING TEST			
		Time showing moderate fitness	
Age	**Heart Rate**	**Men (175 lbs.)[1]**	**Women (125 lbs.)[2]**
20–29	110	17:06–19:36	19:08–20:57
	120	16:36–19:10	18:38–20:27
	130	16:06–18:35	18:12–20:00
	140	15:36–18:06	17:42–19:30
	150	15:10–17:36	17:12–19:00
	160	14:42–17:09	16:42–18:30
	170	14:12–16:39	16:12–18:00
30–39	110	15:54–18:21	17:52–19:46
	120	15:24–17:52	17:24–19:18
	130	14:54–17:22	16:54–18:48
	140	14:30–16:54	16:24–18:18
	150	14:00–16:26	15:54–17:48
	160	13:30–15:58	15:24–17:38
	170	13:01–15:28	14:55–16:54
40–49	110	15:38–18:05	17:20–19:15
	120	15:09–17:36	16:50–18:45
	130	14:41–17:07	16:24–18:18
	140	14:12–16:38	15:54–17:48
	150	13:42–16:09	15:24–17:18
	160	13:15–15:42	14:54–16:48
	170	12:45–15:12	14:25–16:18
50–59	110	15:22–17:49	17:04–18:40
	120	14:53–17:20	16:36–18:12
	130	14:24–16:51	16:06–17:42
	140	13:51–16:22	15:36–17:18
	150	13:26–15:53	15:06–16:48
	160	12:59–15:26	14:36–16:18
	170	12:30–14:56	14:06–15:48
60 +	110	15:33–17:55	16:36–18:00
	120	15:04–17:24	16:06–17:30
	130	14:36–16:57	15:37–17:01
	140	14:07–16:28	15:09–16:31
	150	13:39–15:59	14:39–16:02
	160	13:10–15:30	14:12–15:32

[1]For every 10 lbs. over 175 lbs., men must walk 15 seconds faster to qualify for a fitness category. For every 10 lbs. under 175 lbs., they can walk 15 seconds slower.

[2]For every 10 lbs. over 125 lbs., women must walk 15 seconds faster to qualify for a fitness category. For every 10 lbs. under 125 lbs., they can walk 15 seconds slower.

Used with permission from the Institute for Aerobics Research, Dallas.

your guide. You'll do your heart and lungs the most good if you keep your heart rate at 60 to 80 percent of its maximum for at least 20 minutes three times a week. To find your maximum heart rate, subtract your age from 220.

To track your progress, return to your one-mile test course occasionally. After a few weeks of walking, you should be able to walk the mile faster, or to walk it at the same pace as before without pushing your heart rate as high.

Before taking the fitness test or starting an exercise program, consult your physician. Your doctor might, for example, suggest an exercise stress test to screen for coronary disease.

Source: *Consumer Reports on Health,* August 1991, pp. 60–61.

enhance overall fitness, for example, must be balanced. That is, it must include a variety of exercises that collectively enhance cardiovascular fitness, endurance, strength, flexibility, and body composition. In addition, the intensity, frequency, and duration of these exercises must be carefully established to ensure that the program will help the individual involved meet his or her goals.

The program must also be structured to avoid injury. It should incorporate sufficient time for recovery and rest. Failure to build in adequate intervals for this purpose can result in a phenomenon commonly referred to as "overtraining," whose specifics are not yet well understood. What is clear is that regular rest periods should be provided to prevent the physiological and psychological fatigue that can result from excessive frequency, intensity, or duration. Furthermore, the proper training techniques for each activity must be learned and followed, or the whole training program may be set back for days, weeks, or months. We will discuss the design of training programs in more detail in chapter 5.

Exercise, Fitness, and Health

CHAPTER

3

PARTICIPATION IN AN EXERCISE program can be of considerable benefit to both physical and mental health. We have shown in the previous chapters, however, that the greatest potential health and fitness benefits of exercise can only be realized if exercise is pursued on a consistent basis.

The long-term health benefits of exercise, then, result from improvements in fitness, which in turn are best realized from training. Furthermore, the benefits derived from training are specific to the mode of activity. This is known as the **principle of specificity**. For instance, the effects of strength and flexibility training are clearly specific to the muscles and joints actually involved in the exercise.

An improvement in overall fitness requires a comprehensive, balanced exercise program that addresses all of the major components of fitness. In addition, the nature and magnitude of the health benefits that anyone can expect to receive from exercise are influenced by his or her general level of health and fitness at the beginning of an exercise program.

THE HEALTH BENEFITS OF EXERCISE

In this chapter we focus on the benefits of exercise in promoting health in 4 major areas: blood pressure and hypertension, coronary artery disease, weight control, and mental health.

While we will focus on the areas listed above, several other potential health benefits of a regular exercise program are worth noting here. The possibility that regular exercise may help

Principle of specificity: A basic training principle which states that the benefits derived from training are specific to the mode of activity.

39

FIGURE 3.1
Exercise and Health

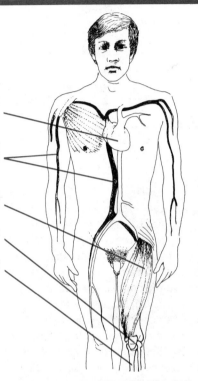

Heart: Aerobic exercise increases the size and stamina of the heart muscle, conditioning the heart to circulate a greater volume of blood with each beat, lowering the risk of heart disease and heart attack.

Circulation: Exercise increases the level of HDL cholesterol in the blood. It lowers blood pressure, which helps prevent stroke and heart attack.

Muscles: Exercise increases the number of capillaries in the muscles, increasing the availability of oxygen to the muscles while strengthening and toning them, and increasing coordination.

Joints: Exercise keeps the joints supple and prevents joint disorders by thickening the cartillage.

Bones: Regular exercise thickens the bones and inhibits loss of calcium from the bones, helping to combat osteoporosis.

Aerobic exercise strengthens the heart, stimulates the building of new blood vessels, which promotes better circulation, and often reduces the level of fat in the blood. Strength and flexibility training benefit the muscles and joints, promoting coordination, increased muscle mass, and bone strength.

Osteoporosis: A chronic disturbance of bone metabolism in which the bone mass decreases and the bones become more fragile; the incidence of osteoporosis increases with age and is greater among women than men.

prevent certain kinds of cancer, for example, is now receiving considerable research and media attention. Other potential health benefits of a regular exercise program include helping reduce the loss of bone mineral associated with **osteoporosis**, helping to prevent back problems by developing a strong back that is resistant to injury, and helping us to maintain good health into old age.

All types of exercise are helpful in promoting good health, but cardiovascular or aerobic exercise seems to be most effective in promoting those physiological changes that have documented

(continued on p. 43)

Heart specialists were among the first to tout the benefits of exercise. Regular aerobic workouts increase the . . . size of the heart and blood vessels, enabling the muscle to pump more blood with less effort. As blood pressure drops, so does the risk of heart disease. But can exercise prevent or reverse other illnesses? The information gathered so far is still sketchy, so most advice is laced with caveats. Still, from curbing diabetes to beating the blues, it looks as though physical exercise is good for what ails you. Here's a sampling of the latest findings:

The Healthy Side Effects of Exercise

Arthritis

Traditionally, doctors have advised people with rheumatoid arthritis—a chronic, severe form of the disease—to avoid vigorous exercise, or risk painful flare-ups of their illness. But new studies from Northwestern University and elsewhere are more encouraging: Four months after beginning a special low-impact aerobics class twice a week, men and women with rheumatoid arthritis reported much less pain, swelling, fatigue, and depression than before they began exercising.

The key, says Northwestern physician Susan Perlman, is creating an individualized exercise program that restores a patient's confidence in his or her physical ability, and builds muscles and endurance without unduly stressing joints.

Cancer

There is some evidence that regular exercise may help ward off certain types of cancer, though researchers still don't know how or to what extent.

Epidemiologists at the Institute for Aerobics Research in Dallas, who recently studied 250,000 veterans, found that men whose occupations required physical activity had lower rates of colon cancer, brain cancer, leukemia, and kidney cancer than sedentary men. Similar research has reinforced the findings, particularly for cancer of the colon. An eight-year study of 2,000 male patients at Roswell Park Memorial Institute in Buffalo, New York, showed that the more men exercised, the lower their incidence of colon cancer. The finding held true even when differences in age, diet, and socio-economic background were taken into account.

In 1985, Harvard University researchers surveyed about 5,000 women aged 21 to 80 and found that the 2,500 who had been athletes in college had a significantly lower incidence of cancer of the breast and reproductive system than women who had not been athletes.

Depression

"It's clear that physical activity is associated with mental health," says Rod K. Dishman, sport psychologist at the University of Georgia in

Athens, "but much remains to be learned about who can benefit from what types of exercise under which circumstances—and why."

For some patients, exercise is apparently as effective as psychotherapy or meditation in relieving moderate depression. In Wisconsin, moderately depressed men and women were randomly assigned to either psychotherapy or running programs. After a year, 11 of the 12 in the running program were no longer depressed while half of those who had received psychotherapy had returned for treatment.

Many doctors already seem sold on the psychological benefits of a workout: A survey of 1,750 physicians published in the *Physician and Sportsmedicine* several years ago indicated that 85 percent prescribe exercise for depression, 60 percent for anxiety, and 43 percent for chemical dependence.

Diabetes

Exercise alone can't curb diabetes, but exercise combined with diet often can. Many of the 10 million Americans who develop diabetes as adults can alleviate their illness simply by watching what they eat and losing excess fat. A vigorous workout also blunts the abnormal rise in blood sugar that diabetics experience after eating carbohydrates, and seems to increase the body's sensitivity to insulin—the chemical that ushers sugar out of the blood and into cells. These effects, however, are reversed by two or three days of inactivity, so researchers urge diabetics to pick a form of exercise they enjoy enough to perform regularly.

Osteoporosis

Three or four hours each week of weight-bearing exercise such as walking or jogging seem to increase bone density in men and women under 30 and slow bone loss in people who are older, according to specialists convened [in 1987] by the National Institutes of Health.

"Most of the advice emphasizes weight-bearing exercise," says Jon Block, bone specialist at the University of California in San Francisco, "but the truth is, osteoporosis is a very complicated disease, and we're just beginning the sort of studies that will tell us how much of what kind of exercise is important. It's possible that swimming is just as good as jogging for preventing brittle bones."

In the meantime, some research indicates that young women who exercise so much that they stop menstruating may increase their risk of osteoporosis later.

—*Deborah Franklin*

Source: *Hippocrates*, January/February 1988, p. 69.

Table 3.1 World Health Organization Criteria for Hypertension

	Normal	Borderline	Hypertension
Systolic	130 mm Hg or less	140–159 mm Hg	160 mm Hg or more
Diastolic	89 mm Hg or less	90–94 mm Hg	95 mm Hg or more

Source: WHO Expert Committee, *Arterial Hypertension* (Geneva: WHO, 1978), WHO Technical Report Series No. 628.

While there is no single "ideal" blood pressure reading, research has shown that increases in blood pressure above a certain level increase the risk of mortality. Shown here is the World Health Organization's scheme for classifying blood pressure readings into 3 ranges—normal, borderline, and hypertension.

Did You Know That . . .

Thomas Jefferson wrote, "Exercise and recreation . . . are as necessary as reading; I will say rather more than necessary, because health is worth more than learning. A strong body makes the mind strong . . . and walking is the best possible exercise."

health benefits. Aerobic exercise appears to help reduce the risk of developing cardiovascular disease, facilitate weight loss, and promote mental health.

The effects of muscular endurance, muscular strength, and flexibility training, on the other hand, tend to be specific to the muscles and joints actually involved in the exercise. Nevertheless, increases in muscular strength and endurance and improvement in the range of motion of joints can increase resistance to injury. They also may slow the decline in function that accompanies advancing age. [1]

Blood Pressure and Hypertension

Hypertension, or high blood pressure, is a primary risk factor for coronary heart disease. As noted in chapter 1, it is also the most common form of cardiovascular disease, affecting an estimated 62 million Americans. [2] While hypertension can affect people of all ages, the highest incidence of hypertension is found among adults, blacks, and those who are obese or overweight. [3] An estimated 10 to 20 percent of adults are affected by hypertension. Among adolescents, the proportion is approximately 1 to 2 percent.

Hypertension is one of the conditions for which exercise has been shown to be a useful treatment tool. Research has shown that cardiovascular training can significantly reduce blood pressure in hypertensive patients and produce at least a slight reduction in those with normal blood pressure values. [4] Specifi-

FIGURE 3.2
Systolic and Diastolic Blood Pressure

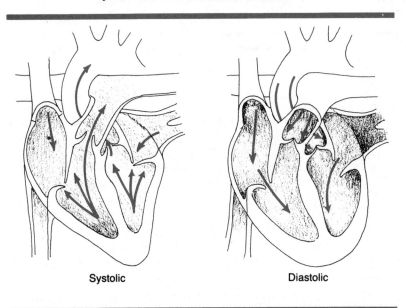

Systolic   Diastolic

The systolic pressure is the maximum pressure attained when the heart contracts and blood is pumped into the arteries. The diastolic blood pressure is the minimum pressure measured when the heart muscle relaxes and fills with blood.

Systolic blood pressure: The blood pressure level in the arteries during the pumping phase of the heartbeat, reflected in the first, or higher, number of the blood pressure reading.

Diastolic blood pressure: The blood pressure level in the arteries during the filling phase of the heartbeat, reflected in the second, or lower, number of the blood pressure reading.

cally, researchers have found an association between increased cardiovascular fitness and a moderate, long-term reduction in both resting **systolic blood pressure** and **diastolic blood pressure**. (Exactly how cardiovascular exercise lowers blood pressure, however, is still unknown.) [5] The magnitude of the improvement in blood pressure level resulting from exercise, however, varies from individual to individual. Among the factors influencing the outcome are age, the nature of the training program, the method of measurement, and other factors specific to the individual such as weight, diet, initial level of fitness, and blood pressure level. [6] In particular, some studies have suggested that exercise is likely to be of greatest value in treating borderline hypertension. [7]

Many doctors now recommend mild cardiovascular exercise for patients with hypertension. It should be noted, however, that

Table 3.2 Recommended Cholesterol Values

Age (yrs)	Cholesterol Level (mg/dl)	
	Moderate Risk	High Risk
2–19	170–185	>185
20–29	201–220	>220
30–39	221–240	>240
40 and over	240–260	>260

Source: Consensus Conference, "Lowering Blood Cholesterol to Prevent Heart Disease," *Journal of the American Medical Association* 251 (1984): 365.

Increased cholesterol levels in the blood have been shown to increase the risk of cardiovascular disease. Shown here are the cholesterol levels established by a National Institute of Health panel to aid in identifying individuals whose cholesterol levels suggest they are in need of treatment.

Did You Know That . . .

In overweight persons, the relative risk for diabetes, hypertension, and hypercholesterolemia is greater at ages 20 through 45 years than at ages 45 through 75 years.

only those whose blood pressure is already well controlled should start an exercise program, and that such a program should be undertaken only under the advice of a physician. The immediate effect of cardiovascular exercise on blood pressure is a substantial rise in systolic blood pressure, and persons whose blood pressure is already dangerously high need to proceed with caution. Further, although exercise can play a significant role in treating hypertension, exercise alone cannot replace drug therapy.

Coronary Heart Disease

As was noted in chapter 1, coronary heart disease is caused by atherosclerosis, the narrowing of the coronary arteries by the formation of plaque on the inside of those blood vessels. Elevated blood cholesterol level is a primary risk factor in the development of atherosclerosis and hence for coronary heart disease.

Cholesterol, also discussed in chapter 1, is one of the two types of fats normally found in the blood. The other type of fat is neutral lipids, or **triglycerides**. Cholesterol, which by itself is insoluble in water, is carried in the blood as part of complex organic compounds called lipoproteins (see chapter 1). The two main forms of cholesterol are **low density lipoprotein cholesterol (LDL)** and **high density lipoprotein cholesterol (HDL)**.

High levels of LDL and triglycerides are associated with an increased risk of developing coronary heart disease. Conversely,

Triglycerides: Fatty compounds found in foods and made in the body, consisting of a carbon "backbone" to which are attached 3 fatty acids.

Low density lipoprotein (LDL) cholesterol: A form of lipoprotein that transports cholesterol and triglycerides in the blood; LDL cholesterol is the so-called "bad cholesterol" that forms deposits on the interior walls of the arteries; high levels of LDL cholesterol are associated with an increased risk of heart disease.

High density lipoprotein (HDL) cholesterol: A form of lipoprotein that transports cholesterol and triglycerides in the blood; HDL cholesterol is the so-called "good cholesterol" that removes LDL cholesterol from the blood; high levels of HDL cholesterol are associated with a reduced risk of heart disease.

FIGURE 3.3
HDL and LDL Cholesterol

LDL
(LOW DENSITY LIPOPROTEIN)

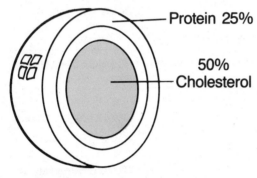

Protein 25%

50% Cholesterol

HDL
(HIGH DENSITY LIPOPROTEIN)

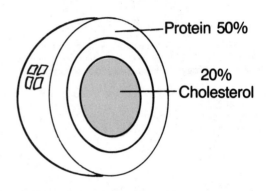

Protein 50%

20% Cholesterol

Source: Leonard Dank/Medical Illustrations.

Low density lipoproteins (LDL) accumulate in the tissues and artery linings and are associated with an increased risk of developing coronary heart disease. High density lipoproteins (HDL) transport the LDL cholesterol away from the tissues and are associated with a decreased level of risk.

high levels of HDL are associated with a decreased level of risk. Apparently, it is the ratio of total cholesterol to HDL that is predictive of the risk of coronary heart disease: the lower the ratio, the lower the level of risk.

It now appears that some types of training result in alterations of blood levels of triglycerides and cholesterol. Blood triglyceride levels in endurance athletes and people who engage in regular aerobic exercise tend to be lower than those in sedentary people. [7] (High-intensity sprint and strength training, on the other hand, appear to have little effect.) [8] Furthermore, regular physical activity appears to retard the increase in triglyceride levels that occurs naturally with age.

There is a significant difference between the effect of aerobic exercise on HDL and its effect on LDL. Considerable evidence shows that cardiovascular endurance training actually raises the blood levels of HDL. [9] This response appears to be related to the

(continued on p. 48)

Exercises for Cardiac Health

Activity	Advantages	Disadvantages	Comment
Walking	Flexible—good for all ages and fitness levels Social Low-impact Accessible Little equipment needed	May not be vigorous enough for young, highly fit individuals	Vastly underrated, an excellent cardiac activity, expecially for individuals over 40
Jogging	Intense enough for all fitness levels	High-impact	Excellent aerobic conditioner
Swimming	Total body conditioner particularly good for upper body Non-impact	Requires specialized facilities Doesn't slow osteoporosis	Particularly good to mix in with jogging for variety
Cycling (stationary or outdoor)	Excellent aerobic conditioner for the heart and lungs Non-impact	Outdoor cycling in urban areas may be dangerous	Modern computerized cycles improve motivation: a health club favorite
Rowing (stationary or outdoor)	Total body conditioner Particularly good for upper body	Requires skill Need specialized facilities or equipment	Excellent stationary rowers make this more accessible
Cross-Country Skiing (stationary or outdoor)	One of the best exercises for using both arms and legs at the same time	Outdoor skiing requires snow	Some of the new cross-country ski machines can make this an excellent indoor workout
Tennis	Vigorous singles tennis burns as many calories per minute as brisk walking	Poor skill level may result in considerable standing around	Assure an aerobic workout by walking to and from the tennis court
Golf	Pleasurable, outdoor activity which involves walking	Considerable stopping and starting The metabolic equivalent of slow walking	Maximize the aerobic benefit—don't ride a cart
Gardening	Enjoyable. Studies show consistent gardening results in lower risk of coronary heart disease	Seasonal in many regions	Don't underestimate this excellent lifelong activity for cardiac health

Activity	Advantages	Disadvantages	Comment
Dancing	Flexible and enjoyable Vigorous dancing is the metabolic equivalent of brisk walking	May need a partner and music	Enjoyment is a key to lifelong, consistent activity
Softball	Competitive and social	Minimal aerobic benefit Requires many other participants	Sorry. The company softball team won't do much for your heart

Source: James M. Rippe, "Heart Health: Special Advertising Section," *Newsweek* (13 February 1989), p. S-16.

amount of activity per week. As little as 10 to 12 miles of jogging per week has produced elevated HDL levels. [10] There are also some reports of elevated HDL levels as a result of a circuit weight-training program. [11] (This kind of training is described in Chapter 5.) In fact, chronic inactivity may actually cause a decrease in HDL levels. [12]

In contrast to its effect on HDL level, aerobic exercise appears to have only a mild effect on LDL levels. Studies have reported decreases in LDL levels of only 10 to 12 percent as a result of cardiovascular exercise, and these decreases appear to occur primarily in persons whose initial LDL levels were significantly higher than normal. [13] Nevertheless, exercise's demonstrated ability to increase HDL levels (and thus to reduce significantly the ratio of total cholesterol to HDL) makes it an effective tool in reducing the risk of coronary heart disease.

Weight Control

Exercise can have considerable benefits for persons trying to control their weight. It has long been prescribed as part of weight-control regimens. The benefits appear at every stage of the weight-loss process.

During dieting, some people experience a decline in their metabolic rate of as much as 20 percent. This decline appears to result from the body's attempt to deal with a reduction in calorie intake by increasing the efficiency with which it uses the calories that are available. The immediate result is a measurable reduction in the number of calories needed to perform basic physiological functions such as muscle contraction, digestion, and respiration. Unless the dieter still further reduces his or her

(continued on p. 50)

Calorie Burners: Activities That Add Up

Activity	Calories Expended (per hour except as noted)	
	Women/120 lbs.	Men/180 lbs.
Aerobic dance	289	391
Backpacking (40 lb. pack)	348	472
Badminton	289	391
Basketball (halfcourt)	255	345
Bicycling (13 mph)	540	840
Bowling	176	240
Canoeing (4 mph)	344	504
Climbing stairs	40/100 steps	45/100 steps
Dancing (ballroom)	238	322
Dancing (rock 'n' roll)	357	483
Football (touch)	255	345
Gardening	220	300
Golf (carrying clubs)	212	288
Gymnastics	263	357
Handball	510	690
Hiking	255	345
Horseback riding	204	276
Jogging (5.5 mph)	552	748
Judo	263	357
Making beds	180	270
Mopping	210	252
Mowing lawn (handmower)	250	320
Ping Pong	204	276
Playing with children	240	320
Pool; billiards	110	150
Racquetball	510	690
Raking leaves and dirt	186	240
Rope jumping	595	805
Rowing (crew)	697	943
Running (10 mph)	765	1035
Sailing	153	207
Scrubbing (walls, tub)	240	300
Shoveling snow	480	600
Skating (ice)	297	403
Skating (roller)	297	403
Skiing (cross country)	595	805
Skiing (downhill)	510	690
Soccer	459	621
Softball (fast pitch)	238	322

Squash	510	690
Surfing	467	633
Swimming (50 yd. per min.)	530	768
Tennis (doubles)	240	360
Tennis (singles)	357	483
Volleyball	297	403
Walking (2 mph)	180	288
Walking (4.5 mph)	330	540
Washing dishes by hand	110	153
Waterskiing	408	552
Weight training	399	541
Wood (chopping or sawing)	350	450

Source: *Hippocrates*, January/February 1988, p. 66.

calorie intake—or increases calorie consumption—the likely longer-term result is an increase in the number of excess calories (calories above and beyond those needed for immediate use). Since any such calories are then stored in the body as fat or **glycogen**, the final outcome is a vicious cycle in which the body's natural response to a reduction in calorie intake significantly retards the progress of weight loss.

Exercise can help interrupt this cycle by increasing calorie consumption. Further, exercise's effects on metabolic rate are not confined to the course of the actual exercise session. Although it has not yet been proven, recent research suggests that the increase in metabolic rate that occurs during the course of an exercise session may persist for a period of time thereafter. [14]

Dieting without exercise can result in a loss of both fat and fat-free mass. Exercise can help to maintain the fat-free mass during dieting, because a greater percentage of the weight loss may come from the body's fat stores. Furthermore, research shows that people who continue to exercise after ending a diet program are less likely to regain their lost weight. In other words, exercise not only helps people lose weight; if continued, it can help them keep weight off. [15]

For the obese, in addition to those benefits associated with weight loss, exercise may exert a positive influence on certain obesity-related disorders, such as high blood pressure, high cholesterol levels, and diabetes. [16]

The obese face several particular problems in creating an exercise program. Aerobic exercise has by far the greatest impact on energy expenditure and is therefore the recommended type of

Glycogen: A form of complex carbohydrate stored in the body, primarily in the liver and muscle tissue.

For a great number of Americans, exercise plays an integral part in their weight loss regimen. However, not all modes of exercise burn calories at the same rate. Those who exercise to lose weight should exercise aerobically—do exercises that increase respiration, heart rate, and intake of oxygen. Aerobic exercise not only improves cardiovascular fitness but is also the most efficient way of expending energy, and thus of burning calories.

Exercise Guidelines for Weight Loss

In exercising for weight loss, balance is the key. Choose a low-impact mode of exercise, such as walking or cycling, to start getting in shape. An out-of-shape person who chooses a high-impact aerobic sport may be setting him- or herself up for injury. Don't underestimate yourself either! Passive exercise machines do not achieve the increased heart rate necessary for an exercise to be aerobic.

The amount of exercise needed for effective weight loss may be intimidating at first. For example, the American College of Sports Medicine recommends exercise that expends 1750 calories per week, which figures out to be 350 calories per session, 5 days a week. This is the equivalent of a 150-pound man walking for 1 hour, 5 times per week. But remember, exercise is about gaining strength and endurance, not about starting at one intensity level and remaining there. Work up to a level of exercise with a calorie expenditure that falls in the range you wish to achieve.

When exercising for weight-loss, you get a break. Weight loss exercising requires sessions whose duration is relatively long, but the intensity required is lower than when exercising for muscle strength and bulk. Aim for a target heart rate in the range of 60 to 70 percent of your maximum heart rate (see "Calculating Your Target Heart Rate" on page 90 in chapter 5), rather than the 60 to 80 percent range commonly recommended for aerobic exercise.

Did You Know That . . .

Foods labeled "diet" or "dietetic" are not necessarily low in calories. The terms simply mean the food has been altered to contain fewer calories, less sodium, or less cholesterol than the regular product.

training. Because low intensity exercise consumes only a nominal number of calories, achieving significant weight loss in a short period of time requires an intensive exercise program—one with fairly lengthy exercise sessions at frequent intervals. Such a program is, however, apt to be initially impractical for most obese people. The extra weight carried by obese people can make activity difficult and uncomfortable. This fact, coupled with their low level of cardiovascular fitness, prevents them from exercising at a high intensity level.

As a result, any exercise-based weight-loss program for the obese should be viewed as a long-term process in which the

(continued on p. 53)

For young and old, regular exercise for the body has some important benefits for the mind, according to two reports from the annual meeting of the American Psychological Association.

TEENAGERS. Exercise serves as a buffer against stressful life events that would otherwise have harmful physical effects. Psychologists followed 200 Los Angeles high school girls for eight months.

Exercise: Getting Your Head in Shape

Some of these girls said they exercised regularly each week and some said they didn't. At the end of the eight-month period, girls who did little exercise and experienced stresses such as moving or a romantic breakup reported high levels of illness and discomfort. Girls who were under similar stresses but exercised regularly reported much less physical illness.

Fitness could prevent illness by minimizing stress-related changes in the cardiovascular system, by increasing people's sense of control over their lives or by providing a respite from stressful situations. "Very likely both physiological and psychological mechanisms are involved," report the investigators, psychologists Jonathon D. Brown of Southern Methodist University and Judith M. Siegel of the University of California, Los Angeles.

ELDERS. Exercise may lead to improved memory, reasoning ability and reaction time. Researchers at Scripps College compared 42 men and women who exercised vigorously for at least 75 minutes each week with a similar group who exercised for less than 10 minutes weekly.

Psychologists Louis Clarkson-Smith and Alan A. Hartley had these people—aged 55 to 89—complete a range of mental tests, from reciting a list of numbers backward to solving verbal analogies. The high-exercise group showed better memories, quicker reactions and more accurate reasoning, even after differences in age and education were taken into account.

Although the researchers concede that the high-exercise group may have been more healthy to begin with and that their superior mental abilities could stem from this overall better health, they believe that regular exercise by older people may forestall some of the degenerative effects of aging on the central nervous system.

—*Joshua Fischman*

Source: *Psychology Today*, January 1988, p. 14.

duration and intensity of the program are increased gradually and prudently. Such a program, coupled with an appropriate reduction in calorie intake, can produce significant weight loss benefits over a period of months. However, exercise should not be thought of as a cure for obesity.

A suitable exercise program for an obese person includes lower-impact aerobic activities performed at moderate intensities. Low-impact choices such as cycling and walking are suggested, due to the added stress that obesity places on the musculoskeletal system. Additional guidelines are suggested in "Exercise Guidelines for Weight Loss" on page 51.

Mental Health

Exercise and improved physical fitness have demonstrable psychological benefits for many adults, and there are beneficial emotional effects across all ages and for both sexes. Exercise has been associated with an improved sense of well-being [17], better quality of sleep [18], and reduced muscle tension. [19] Interestingly, the psychological benefits of exercise may be the greatest for those persons whose initial physical and psychological fitness is the lowest. [20]

Physical fitness has also been shown to be positively associated with lower levels of anxiety and stress [21] and with reduced levels of mild to moderate depression. [22] Appropriate exercise can reduce neuromuscular tension, help lower an elevated resting heart rate, and reduce the blood level of some "stress" hormones. Some researchers believe that exercise can assist in stress management and that the improved self-image resulting from exercise can help bolster the internal resources needed to deal with stress and tensions.

It is important to realize that the associations between exercise and mental health found by researchers are just that, associations, and do not imply causation. In other words, it is currently possible to say only that exercise is associated with these mental health benefits, not that it is directly responsible for them.

COMMON MYTHS ABOUT EXERCISE

We have briefly discussed some of the health benefits of following a regular exercise program. While it is essential to keep them in mind, it is also important to recognize myths about exercise. Exaggerated or incorrect information about exercise can cause

(continued on p. 55)

Did You Know That . . .

The weight-gaining years are those between 25 and 34, says a Department of Health and Human Services study. Women are twice as likely as men to show major gains (30 pounds or more) in those years. After age 55, weight begins to drop.

Years ago, bodybuilder Charles Atlas preyed on insecure adolescents through comic-book ads that promised to transform 98-pound weaklings into hulking he-men. Today, the exercise business is still flourishing, and so are the myths. Here are some of the most enduring myths about exercise:

Myth: You can burn fat from specific areas by exercising those spots.

Fitness: Working Out the Facts

There's no such thing as "spot reduction." When you exercise, you use energy produced by burning fat in all parts of your body—not just around the muscles that are doing the most work. So sit-ups won't take fat off your abdomen any faster than off your hips or thighs. However, sit-ups can strengthen your abdominal muscles, which may help hold your [stomach] in.

Myth: The more you sweat, the more fat you lose.

If you exercise in extreme heat or in a plastic "weight-loss suit," you will indeed sweat and lose weight. But sweat reflects lost water, not lost fat. So those pounds will return when you replenish fluids through food and drink. You could also suffer heat exhaustion if you push yourself too hard in extreme heat or in plastic clothes, which don't allow sweat to evaporate.

How heavily you sweat is not a good measure of how much energy you're using. Sweating depends more on temperature, humidity, lack of conditioning, body weight, and individual variability.

Myth: Exercise defeats a weight-loss diet because it increases your appetite.

People don't necessarily become hungrier when they start exercising. In fact, some evidence suggests that exercise can even depress appetite for a short while. Those who do eat more when they exercise usually add fewer calories than they burn in their workouts.

For example, a recent study published in the American Journal of Clinical Nutrition evaluated 20 men and women who exercised on a treadmill for an hour on each of five consecutive days and then went without exercise for another five. The women's caloric intake stayed about the same over the 10 days, while each bout on the treadmill burned some 400 calories. The men added an average of 200 calories to their diets on exercise days, but each workout burned almost 600 calories.

There's also evidence that exercise can temporarily raise your metabolic rate, so you continue to burn calories faster for several hours after a workout.

Myth: Exercise isn't much good for trimming down, since you gain weight in muscle anyway.

Aerobic exercises, such as bicycling, jogging, and swimming, burn fat more than they add muscle. With exercises like weight lifting, the muscle you gain may indeed weigh more than the fat you burn. But you may still become slimmer, since the added muscle is denser and less bulky than the lost fat. And the few extra pounds of muscle don't carry the health risks of excess fat.

Myth: Building muscles reduces flexibility.

If you lift weights without moving your joints through their full range of motion, you can indeed lose flexibility. But weight training can actually improve flexibility if you do move your joints fully. Stretch before and after using weights (a good idea with any exercise program) to help keep you limber. . . .

Myth: No pain, no gain.

Exercise doesn't have to hurt to do good. You're bound to feel some burning in your muscles when you begin or intensify an exercise program. But once you've worked up to a regular routine of aerobic exercise, you needn't continually push yourself beyond that level to benefit. In fact, recent research suggests that you can benefit from less vigorous exercise than was previously thought necessary. . . .

To avoid pain during and after exercise, intensify your workouts slowly. Begin each session with a warmup: Jog in place, ride a stationary bicycle, or do calisthenics for a few minutes. After your muscles are warm and your heart is beating faster, stop and stretch. That improves flexibility and helps prevent injury. Stretch only until you feel tension, not pain. After your workout, cool down to keep blood from "pooling" in your legs: Continue what you've been doing, but at a slower pace a few minutes. Then stretch again.

Source: *Consumer Reports Health Letter,* July 1991, pp. 49–52.

Did You Know That . . .

One study provides evidence that regular exercise can dramatically improve your love life, whether you're 40, 60, or older. The same study also shows that too much exercise diminishes sexual appetite.

more harm than good; it can even hamper or derail the most committed person's exercise program. Some of the more common mistaken beliefs about exercise are discussed in "Fitness: Working Out the Facts" above.

One of these, which bears repeating here, is the so-called **spot reduction myth**. Many people are under the mistaken impression that performing muscular endurance-type exercises for a specific muscle group results in removal of the *subcutaneous fat* (fat stored just under the surface of the skin) over that muscle. However, any fat the body uses for fuel is obtained from deposits throughout the body rather than from any fat deposits over the exercising muscle. Ironically, because such exercises (situps and leg lifts, for example) do not require a substantial amount of energy as compared to aerobic exercise, they may in fact be a poor exercise choice for those whose primary goal is weight loss.

(continued on p. 57)

Spot reduction myth: The unfounded belief that exercising specific portions of the body will result in the loss of subcutaneous storage fat in those areas.

FIGURE 3.4
The Spot Reduction Myth

The spot reduction myth says that selectively exercising a particular area ("spot") of the body will result in a loss of fat in that area, the thighs, for example. Research has conclusively demonstrated, however, that this is not true. While exercise is always valuable, no exercise will cause fat to be lost from just one area of the body.

Probably the most harmful myth about exercise is the belief that it can cure all ills, from excess fat to heart disease. Yes, exercise can enhance health by reducing the risk of certain diseases, by helping to treat obesity, and by promoting mental health. But it cannot work miracles.

The fact remains that many factors play a role in good health. Among them are controlling stress, not smoking, and getting proper rest and nutrition. Exercise is but one of several factors needed to help us achieve our goal: wellness. W

Did You Know That . . .

It is a dangerous myth that exercise has to hurt to be of benefit. Pain is a sign of overuse and possible injury and should be heeded.

C H A P T E R

4

Exercise Risks and Precautions

Taking precautions—including allowing for such factors as weather, temperature, fatigue, muscular or joint soreness, and equipment condition—is an essential facet of any training program. Despite its justifiably positive image, exercise is not without risks.

Virtually every form of exercise has its own potential hazards. No one should pursue any form of training without being aware of them. Failing to take proper precautions can make training less effective. It can also cause discomfort, injury, illness, and even death.

In this chapter, we identify exercise risks and precautions. We provide this information not to discourage you from exercising, but to ensure that your exercise experience is as safe, comfortable, and positive as possible.

ENVIRONMENTAL RISK FACTORS: HEAT AND COLD

It may seem surprising, but extreme environmental temperatures, both heat and cold, present the most common and dangerous risks associated with exercise. They are, perhaps, also the most underestimated, or overlooked, risks. Fortunately, simple precautions—using common sense, proper clothing, and adequate hydration—can prevent most of the difficulties you may encounter.

Exercising in the Heat
Heat is probably the most common environmental hazard likely to be encountered when exercising. Some heat-related conditions

FIGURE 4.1
The Sweating Process

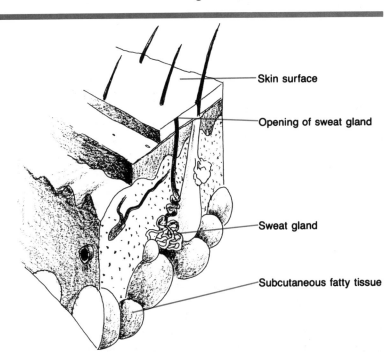

Skin surface

Opening of sweat gland

Sweat gland

Subcutaneous fatty tissue

Sweat glands beneath the surface of the skin are filled with saline fluid. As the internal body temperature rises, this fluid is transported to the skin surface. The body temperature lowers as the perspiration evaporates.

or illnesses, like heat rash, are minor and may cause nothing but temporary discomfort. Others, such as heatstroke, may be quite serious. Common heat-related illnesses are identified and described later in the chapter.

Under normal conditions, the human body's **thermoregulatory** (heat-regulating) processes maintain its **core temperature** (internal temperature) within the range needed for proper metabolic functioning. This is vital because the body's basic metabolic and other physiological processes can only be carried out within a very narrow temperature range. In fact, the human body can tolerate a variation of only about 4 degrees Centigrade in core temperature without suffering impairment in physical and mental performance. [1]

Thermoregulatory: Refers to the body's heat-regulating processes, which maintain the body's core temperature at the level needed for proper metabolic functioning.

Core temperature: The body's internal temperature, normally maintained at about 37 degrees centigrade (98.6 degrees Fahrenheit).

Hyperthermia: A condition characterized by an excessively high body temperature. Hyperthermia may be accompanied by the symptoms of heat exhaustion or heatstroke.

Hypothermia: A condition characterized by a subnormal body temperature. The symptoms of hypothermia include drowsiness and significantly reduced respiratory and heart rates.

Convection: The transfer of heat from a warmer to a cooler portion of a fluid or gas as a result of a current or movement, as when heat generated in the muscles during exercise is transferred to the surface of the body by the movement of the blood.

Conduction: A thermoregulatory process by which heat is transferred from a warmer to a cooler object when the two come in contact.

Radiation: A thermoregulatory process by which heat is transferred from a warmer to a cooler area even in the absence of direct physical contact; heat may be radiated away from the body, for example, when the temperature of the surrounding air is cooler than that of the body.

Evaporation: The process by which a liquid is converted to a gas, giving up heat in the process; the evaporation of perspiration from the surface of the skin is one of the body's natural thermoregulatory mechanisms.

Excessively high core temperature is called **hyperthermia**. Excessively low core temperature is termed **hypothermia**. Either condition can quickly lead to a decline in performance or endurance and, if left unchecked, even to death.

Heat is generated by the muscles during normal activity, as the energy derived from food is transformed into work. This excess heat is transferred from the muscles to the skin, by means of an increase in blood flow to the skin. It is then removed from the body by means of one of 4 processes: convection, conduction, radiation, or evaporation.

Convection occurs when moving air (such as a breeze) removes heat from the body. Heat may also be removed from the body by **conduction**—coming into contact with a cooler object, e.g., sitting on a cool chair. If the temperature of the body is warmer than that of the surrounding air, heat may be lost through **radiation**. Finally, heat may be removed from the body by the **evaporation** of sweat. [2] The last of these, the sweating process, is particularly important, accounting for up to 80 percent of heat loss. [3]

Any increase in muscular activity increases the need of the muscles involved for oxygen. As a result, the blood flow to the working muscles increases during exercise, regardless of environmental temperature. Under a heavy workload, the increased demand for blood by the muscles can take precedence over demands from other parts of the body, resulting in less blood being available for skin circulation. This reduces the skin's ability to remove excess body heat, and in turn to a buildup in body heat. The intensity of exercise is a critical factor in determining the amount of excess heat generated by the body. The higher the intensity, the more heat the muscles produce.

Intense exercise on a hot or even moderately warm day, particularly when the humidity is high, can result in a potentially dangerous situation. Under such conditions, the heat generated by the muscles can exceed the body's cooling capacity, leading to an increase in core temperature. This is because high environmental temperatures render ineffective all of the body's normal cooling mechanisms except sweating. Furthermore, high humidity conditions, when the air is nearly saturated with water, greatly inhibit the evaporation of moisture from the skin that is central to the sweating process. Thus, instead of evaporating, sweat merely remains on the skin without producing any cooling effect. Intense exercise in the heat can quickly create the conditions that lead to heat exhaustion or heatstroke, and great caution should be used when exercising under such conditions.

(continued on p. 63)

At Roosevelt Hospital in New York City, which lies a few blocks from the southern end of Central Park, the medical staff is accustomed to seeing four or five cases of heatstroke each summer.

"One of those cases is usually an elderly person who was baking in his or her apartment," said Dr. Patrick Griffin, Roosevelt's associate director of medical service. "The other two or three or four are runners brought in from Central Park."

When It's Too Hot to Handle Exercise

The recent deaths of two men in their early 20's from heatstroke after participating in Central Park in the Manufacturers Hanover Corporate Challenge series of foot races, which began at 7 P.M., are a chilling reminder of our vulnerability anytime we exercise outdoors in the summer. One of the victims, Anthony Mezzina, 24 years old, was overweight and out of . . . shape, and the other, David Reynolds, 23, said before his condition worsened that he had not run more than a mile since high school.

Those of us who are fit might be tempted toward smugness about running in the heat. But the ugly truth is that heat exhaustion—the first stage in the body's overheating—and then heatstroke when some of the body's major systems shut down and death becomes likely, can catch even the most seasoned athlete by surprise. Indeed, a third runner, a 28-year-old woman who ran 30 to 40 miles a week, was hospitalized after the Aug. 4 [1988] race in Central Park with heat exhaustion. She recovered.

"We need to recognize that we have limits," said Lawrence E. Armstrong, a Ph.D. research physiologist in the heat research division of the Army's Institute of Environmental Medicine in Natick, Mass. "Everyone is a potential heatstroke victim if you run on a severe enough day and at a hard enough exercise intensity."

Two of the most often repeated adages by sports doctors, trainers and physiologists are "Know your body" and "Listen to your body."

Probably the most critical element in knowing your body's needs in the heat involves **dehydration.** Evaporation of sweat from the skin is the body's main cooling system, and this lost water must be constantly replaced. But dehydration can mount faster than expected. The first obvious warning signs can appear only after the problem is quite advanced.

Every person who exercises in the summer should have an accurate notion of how much fluid he loses during particular types of exercise. The typical sweat rate is 1 to 1.5 quarts an hour. Your own rate is easy to determine. Weigh yourself without clothes before beginning an exercise session and then weigh yourself without clothes afterward and note the weight loss per unit of time. A weight loss of 2 pounds an hour represents four 8-ounce glasses of water you should drink for each hour of exercise.

Dehydration: A reduction in body fluid level (including blood volume) resulting from a failure to maintain fluid intake at a level sufficient to replace fluids lost through sweating and other thermo-regulatory mechanisms; the early signs of dehydration include lethargy, anxiety, and irritability; severe dehydration can result in a loss of coordination and unconsciousness.

But there are many factors that cause heatstroke, and they vary widely from person to person.

Poor physical fitness is a prime cause. Overweight is another. Someone who is not fit lacks the aerobic conditioning that permits the heart to pump enough blood carrying oxygen to muscle cells and to meet the body's myriad other demands during exercise. The added weight means that more internal heat is generated as the body exercises because more weight must be carried around.

This combination can spell trouble enough on a cool day when heat is more readily carried away from the surface of the skin. But on a hot day, particularly if it is humid, far less heat is dissipated because body heat generated by exercise can be carried away only through evaporation, and when the temperature and humidity are high, evaporation is severely limited. In such conditions, the internal heat buildup can be dangerous.

Dr. Armstrong said that recent followup studies of heatstroke victims in the Army found wide variability among the causes of their collapse.

Some people have bodies that exhibit a low work economy—that is, they produce more internal heat for a given amount of work—and as a result are more vulnerable. Others are more vulnerable because of a recent viral or bacterial illness.

Advancing age is another factor, because with mounting years the ability to sweat declines and the body's ability to take up oxygen and use it to fuel the muscle cells declines. Aerobic conditioning, however, greatly lessens this possibility.

Medications, particularly sedatives and antihistamines, can also predispose someone to develop heatstroke. Some skin disorders, such as heat rashes, can clog sweat glands and reduce the overall cooling caused by sweating.

Finally, even a very fit runner who always runs in the cool of dawn and is not acclimated to running in the heat of the day could run into trouble. Heat acclimitization is very important and a gradual introduction to running in the heat should begin at least two weeks before the full force of exercising in the heat is to be experienced.

In the end, however, common sense is essential. When the temperature of the air approaches or exceeds 90 degrees and the humidity is above 75 percent, loud alarm bells should ring before beginning exercise, whether you plan a run, a tennis match or a fast-paced bicycle ride. If you do not check the weather before exercise, you are courting trouble.

Listen to your body. Are you properly conditioned? Are you properly hydrated? Do you feel well, or is a cold coming on or have you just recovered from an illness? Soldiers in excellent condition who suffered heatstroke during exertion in the heat often reported that they did not feel well before the exertion began, Dr. Armstrong said.

Mankind, alas, has always sought to prove his physical prowess. A corporate challenge footrace is another way of pitting oneself against the saber-toothed tiger. On this subject, let Dr. Griffin, who helped attend the deaths of the two heatstroke victims, have the last word.

"I think the problem with the corporate challenge race is really peer pressure," he said. "These kids who may or may not be athletic are coerced by their office mates to go out and run for the team. I'm sure they went out there saying it's only a few miles and if you get through it you get points for our team.

"To be unconditioned and unused to running in such weather conditions is foolish."

Source: William Stockton, *New York Times* (15 August 1988), p. C-10.

Did You Know That . . .

Despite the popularity of sports drinks, water is the most beneficial drink there is, especially during exercise. That is because the body needs water more than it needs the minerals and carbohydrates in sports drinks.

One consequence of the body's heavy dependence on the sweating process for cooling during exercise is that its fluid reserves can be depleted, a condition called dehydration. Severe dehydration can lead to a loss of blood volume. In the heat, it is not uncommon to lose up to 2 liters of sweat during a 1-hour session of aerobic exercise. Unless the lost fluids are replaced promptly to maintain adequate blood volume, the blood flow to the skin will be decreased, and sweat production will be reduced. If this condition is allowed to continue unchecked, the body's ability to dissipate heat will be greatly reduced and its thermoregulatory capacity severely compromised.

When this occurs, the core temperature will rise at an extremely rapid rate. At this point, the symptoms of hyperthermia begin to appear: sluggishness, lightheadedness, and a rapid or irregular heartbeat. These symptoms suggest that the functioning of the thermoregulatory system has been impaired, or even that it has shut down altogether. This is a potentially life-threatening condition, and anyone with such symptoms should be attended to immediately.

Heat Illnesses   As mentioned earlier, there are many forms of heat illness. They range in severity from dehydration and its various symptoms, such as dizziness and cramping, to heat exhaustion and heatstroke.

- *Dehydration.* This is a condition in which lost fluid is not adequately replaced. It may result in a decreased blood volume and an **electrolyte** imbalance, and is sometimes accompanied by dizziness and cramping. Dizziness is caused by insufficient blood flow to the brain resulting from either low blood volume

Electrolyte: A substance such as sodium, calcium, magnesium, or potassium, which is normally present in the body and carries an electrical charge (either positive or negative) when in solution. A correct balance of electrolytes is necessary for proper cell function.

Table 4.1 Effects of Dehydration on the Body

Percent Body Weight Lost	Symptoms
2.0	Thirst, discomfort, performance impairment
3.0	Dry mouth, decreased urination
5.0	Difficulty concentrating
8.0	Dizziness, labored breathing, confusion
10.0	Spastic muscles, loss of balance, delirium
11.0	Circulatory insufficiency

It is important to replace any fluids lost due to dehydration during exercise by drinking cool water or a dilute electrolyte solution. Increasing levels of dehydration—as measured in percentage of body weight lost—have progressively more serious effects on the body, and can, if left unchecked, be very harmful.

or excessive dilation of blood vessels, either of which can result in a drop in blood pressure. Cramping (heat cramps) is a condition characterized by painful, severe, and involuntary muscle contractions (spasms) that are probably caused by an electrolyte imbalance associated with heavy sweating.

- *Heat exhaustion.* This condition is brought about by exercise (especially in the heat). The major symptoms are profuse sweating, dizziness, fatigue, cramping, and nausea. Heat exhaustion may be caused by an excessively high core temperature, excessive water loss (water depletion/heat exhaustion), or excessive salt loss (salt depletion/heat exhaustion).
- *Anhidrotic heat exhaustion.* This is a more serious form of heat exhaustion that occurs when the body has ceased sweating, despite an elevated core temperature. This is a direct precursor to heatstroke. The symptoms are similar to those of heat exhaustion, accompanied by a body temperature of 38 to 40 degrees Centigrade (100 to 104 degrees Fahrenheit).
- *Heatstroke* is the most serious heat illness. The symptoms are often similar to those of heat exhaustion, and the two conditions may be difficult to distinguish in some instances. Heatstroke is characterized by an extremely high core temperature of 41 degrees Centigrade or higher (106 degrees Fahrenheit), often accompanied by a virtual collapse of the body's thermoregulatory mechanism. The symptoms include mental disorientation,

unsteady gait, hot, dry skin, a rapid pulse, and unconscious. Unless treated promptly, it can be fatal, and prompt medical attention should be sought for anyone suffering from heatstroke symptoms.

All forms of heat illness, and especially heatstroke, involve a significant rise in core body temperature that must be lowered. This may be done by resting in a cool place or by the immediate administration of fluids, drinking water, and electrolyte replacement. In extreme cases where the subject is semi- or unconscious, fluids should not be administered orally because of the danger of choking. In such cases, emergency personnel may administer an ice-water bath accompanied by intravenous fluid replacement. It should be emphasized, however, that severe heat illness, and particularly heatstroke, is a medical emergency requiring prompt treatment by a physician or other trained health-care person.

Precautions Fortunately, heat illness can often be prevented by taking simple precautions. In order to combat dehydration and its consequences, all of which can occur even at moderate temperatures, one of the most important precautions is simply to drink plenty of plain, cool water.

It is important to note that one's sense of thirst does not always keep pace with the body's need for fluid. It is critical, therefore, to drink water before, during, and after exercise in the heat, particularly if the exercise session is relatively long. A good rule of thumb is to drink at least one large glass (500 ml) of water before exercise and one every 20 minutes during activity. After exercise, it is crucial to consume fluids to ensure adequate rehydration. A person whose body weight is stable and who is voiding dilute, clear urine at least twice a day is considered *fully hydrated*.

Although sweating while exercising in the heat results in a loss of electrolytes such as sodium, the use of salt tablets to replace sodium is not usually recommended. In cases of mild to moderate sweating, the normal intake of salt in food will usually provide adequate sodium replacement.

Exercising in the Cold
Exercise in very cold environmental conditions presents risks quite different from those associated with exercise in the heat. The major problem with cold weather is that the body can lose heat to the environment faster than muscle activity can generate it. If that happens, core temperature can drop, leading to hypothermia.

Did You Know That . . .

Soft drinks with more than 10 percent sugar content slow down absorption of the fluid by the body, and may cause abdominal cramps, nausea, and diarrhea.

When the body encounters cold temperatures, several physiological mechanisms are activated to prevent heat loss and maintain core temperature. The primary response is a reduction in the blood flow to the skin, hands, and feet, and a shunting of blood to the core of the body (the trunk or torso) to protect vital

(continued on p. 68)

FIGURE 4.2

The Hazards of Heat and Humidity

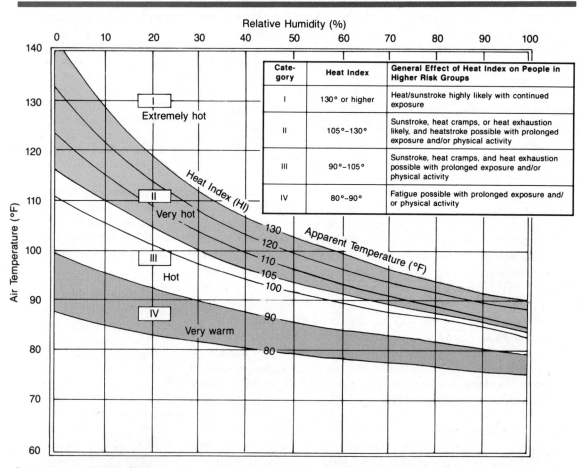

Source: National Weather Service.

To determine the risk of exercising in the heat, locate the outside air temperature on the left-hand scale and the relative humidity on the horizonal scale. Where these two lines cross is the apparent temperature or heat index. For example, on a 90° day with 70% humidity, the heat index registers 105°. This would not be a safe day to exercise outdoors.

Winter—A Great Time for Exercise

Cold weather doesn't have to mean the end of outdoor exercise for most people. Running, cycling, and walking in winter can, like skiing, be exhilarating. They're also good ways to get out into the sunlight and thus help you avoid wintertime blues. The trick is to make allowances for the weather.

Dress Right

Don't overdress. The most common problem isn't that exercisers wear too little clothing in the cold, but too much. Exercise raises body temperature significantly—even a moderate workout can make you feel that it's 30° warmer than it really is. So when you're about to run on a 25° day, dress for about 55°.

Wear several layers of loose-fitting thin clothing. This helps insulate you and trap the heat you generate. And you'll be able to take off layers if you become too warm. When you remove a garment, tie it around your waist or put it in a day pack.

First layer: Start with underwear made of a fabric that draws sweat away from your skin (such as polypropylene, Capilene, or Thermax). In contrast, cotton holds moisture next to your skin, making you feel cold and clammy. Wet clothes draw heat away from you.

Middle layers: Next can come a wool sweater, synthetic turtleneck, and/or pile jacket. It's easy to keep legs warm: wear sweat pants or tights, with leg warmers or thermal long johns when it's really cold.

Outer layer: Wear a jacket that's waterproof, wind-resistant, and yet breathable (so that moisture isn't trapped inside). Synthetics like Gore-Tex fit the bill. An ordinary windbreaker is okay for a short workout in dry weather.

Zip 'em up. Zippers make clothes adaptable: when you get too hot you can unzip them halfway to let in air, and you can remove garments easily. In general it's best to start opening zippers and/or removing layers *as soon as you start to sweat.* Tie a small loop of string or fabric to each zipper so that you can pull it open without having to take off your mittens or gloves.

Mittens or gloves? Mittens are warmer than gloves since they keep your fingers together and have less surface area from which heat can escape. In very cold weather, the added warmth from mittens is worth the loss in dexterity. You can also wear special inner liners made of polypropylene or another material that draws sweat from your skin.

Cap it off. Oddly enough, one way to keep your feet warm is to wear a hat, since you lose so much heat through your head. Your best bet is a wool or synthetic cap or a hood. Another option is a cap that folds down into a face mask in case the wind starts gusting or it begins to snow (make sure it doesn't obscure your vision or hearing). To get a cap to fit under a bike helmet, you may have to remove a few of the pads inside the helmet.

Shoes. Wear shoes that offer good traction and shock absorption, especially when running on hard, frozen ground. Shoes should have a little extra space inside to trap warm air and, when it's really cold, let you wear an extra pair of socks.

The Easy Way Outdoors

Warm up and stretch. It's a good idea to first warm up (such as jogging in place) and stretch indoors and then perhaps stretch again outside. When you've finished exercising, cool down and stretch indoors.

Drink as much in the cold as in the heat. This is crucial. It's easy to become dehydrated in cold weather because of the water you lose from sweating and breathing (you have to warm and moisten the cold air you inhale), and because of your stepped-up urine production. Dehydration hinders your body's ability to regulate its temperature. Drink before, during, and after your workout. Skip alcohol and caffeine; both dehydrate you. Drinking alcohol also gives you the illusion of warmth while it robs you of heat by causing blood vessels near the skin's surface to dilate.

Compensate for the wind. The wind can penetrate clothes and remove the insulating layer of warm air around the body. When the temperature is 20°, a 15-mph wind makes it feel like −5° (this is called the wind-chill factor). And fast motion, as in cycling or skiing, has the same effect as the wind since it increases air movement past the body. *Tip:* compensate for a strong wind by running or riding against it on your way out, then with it behind you on the way back. That way you'll get the worst over before you're tired and sweaty.

Be on the defensive. Shorter daylight hours, poor weather visibility, plus the risk of skidding cars call for careful running, walking, and cycling.

Keep moving. If you stop exercising for any reason and remain outdoors, put on extra clothes *before* you start to feel cold. To stay warm, try to keep moving.

Snow! Ice! Though some joggers manage to run in even the worst weather without injury, exercising on snow or ice is not worth the risk. One exception: some people are able to run reasonably well on hard, packed snow, provided they slow their pace, take smaller steps, and wear shoes with good traction. Wet snow and ice, however, are extremely treacherous, so in such weather it's safest to exercise indoors.

Wear sunglasses and sunscreen. Snow-covered ground can reflect the sun and thus burn your face and obscure your vision, especially at high altitudes.

When to come in from the cold

Who shouldn't exercise in cold weather? Breathing cold air is not harmful to healthy people; you can't "freeze your lungs." However, it can be risky for those who suffer from angina, asthma, or high blood pressure—they should check with a doctor before exercising in the cold. For such people, wearing a ski mask or scarf pulled loosely in front of the face may help warm up inhaled air.

Frostbite and hypothermia. These are the two main dangers of exercising in the cold. Dressing properly and taking other precautions described here are your best safeguards. Be on guard for the numbness and white discoloration of frostbite—particularly on your hands, ears, toes, and face. Cyclists and runners have also reported cases of penile frostbite, so consider wearing an extra pair of shorts. Hypothermia, which involves a dangerous drop in body temperature, is mostly a risk when you're out in very cold weather for many hours, especially if you're wet, injured, and/or not moving around enough to stay warm.

Source: *University of California Berkeley Wellness Letter,* December 1989, p. 6.

---

organs such as the heart from freezing. [4] Whereas cold fingers or feet can be uncomfortable, or may even lead to frostbite, a significant decrease in core body temperature is invariably fatal. Thus the body's natural response to cold is perfectly rational from a survival standpoint. The nature of this response is such, however, that cold is a particular problem for small or thin people and for small children, whose greater ratio of surface area to body mass makes them lose heat faster.

Another hazard associated with cold weather is an elevation of blood pressure. Inhalation of cold air induces a reflex mechanism that can cause the coronary arteries (the arteries that supply blood to the heart muscle) to constrict. [5] It may also lead to constriction of the bronchial tubes in the lungs. This makes cold-weather exercise, such as snow shoveling, of particular risk to people with coronary artery disease as well as to those with respiratory problems such as asthma.

Precautions Even though exercise increases the body temperature, protective clothing is still necessary in cold conditions. Wearing several thin layers during exercise, rather than one thick one, is often recommended. Layers can be removed as body temperature rises, or replaced gradually when remaining outdoors after exercise. This will allow for careful regulation of body temperature and sweating.

Since the insulating qualities of most clothing material are adversely affected by moisture, once the layers become wet the body may begin to chill. To keep moisture away from the skin, therefore, the layer of clothing closest to the skin should be made of a quick-drying material. Synthetic fibers that transfer moisture away from the skin, such as polypropylene, are best for this purpose. The other layers should be designed to maintain body heat and block wind without promoting an accumulation of sweat. Wool, which retains much of its insulating power even when damp, is an excellent second layer.

The hands and especially the head are major sources of heat loss and should be kept covered when you are exercising in cold temperatures. Up to one-half of the body's heat loss at lower temperatures is through the head. Failure to protect the extremities is an invitation to frostbite. Especially at risk are the fingers, toes, and nose.

Even in the cold, dehydration from sweating is a concern, as is loss of moisture through breathing dry, cold air, which readily extracts moisture from the body. The same rules for adequate hydration apply as for exercise in the heat, although the degree of concern, naturally, is not as great.

RISKS OF INJURY FROM TRAINING

Apart from the external, environmental dangers, there are a variety of other risks associated with exercise. The most common problems are those which result from inconsistency in training, imbalanced training, **overtraining**, and competitive training. Misuse of or improperly maintained equipment may also create

Overtraining: A term synonymous with exercising at an excessive level of intensity, frequency, or duration, which often leads to injury, pain, or excessive fatigue.

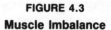
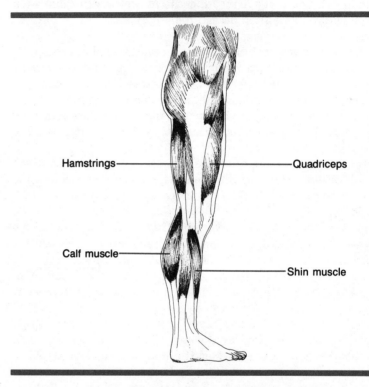

A runner's leg will often have relatively highly developed hamstrings and calf muscles in comparison with the muscles in the front of the leg (quadriceps and shin). While this is a natural result of sustained running, the resulting disparity in the relative strength of the 2 sets of muscles, if left uncorrected, can increase the risk of injury when engaging in other activities.

risks. Another common cause is inappropriate clothing and other exercise gear.

All of these potential risks are discussed in this section, along with appropriate treatment methods for some of the more common exercise-related injuries.

Inconsistent Training, Imbalanced Training, and Overtraining

A carefully designed, disciplined approach to training is important not only for its fitness benefits but as a means of reducing injury risk. For a variety of reasons, many people become erratic in their exercise patterns. The danger comes when, perhaps out of frustration over their failure to achieve desired results within a certain period of time, they then try to make up for lost time by exercising too frequently, at too high an intensity, or for too long. Injury often follows. Sporadic, inconsistent participation in exercise also slows improvements in fitness. Inconsistent training can even eliminate any training effect.

One frequent cause of injury is overtraining. Overtraining is particularly common at the onset of an exercise program. Although the specifics of this phenomenon are not well understood – and some experts even dispute that there is such a thing – it occurs most frequently when an attempt to meet a specific training goal leads to exercise sessions that are too long with insufficient rest. [6] Developing a reasonable exercise program and sticking with it are two of the best strategies you can use to prevent injury.

Competitive Training
Many people, when setting their personal training goals, like to choose a competition such as a foot race, bike race, or triathlon as a trial or benchmark for their improvement in fitness. This can, in some instances, lead to problems. Training for fitness and training for competition are not the same thing. Competitive athletes often push themselves to the extremes of their training capabilities because they wish to excel. Some also tend to place a heavy emphasis on the training that is most directly related to their chosen event. Some runners, for example, may ignore muscular strength or flexibility training. Bodybuilders and weight lifters may emphasize strength training at the expense of aerobic training. By doing so, they may risk injury and overtraining symptoms such as soreness or extreme fatigue.

For the average person who just wants to compete for fun while increasing fitness, training extremes are unnecessary and unwise. A healthy approach to competition is consistent with the balanced approach to fitness taken in this book. In the end, the results of such an approach are likely to be satisfying and achieved with a minimal risk of injury.

Common Training Injuries and Their Treatment
Most training injuries are minor, temporary, and easily treated. Using common sense following an injury can prevent it from becoming aggravated and becoming more serious. [7] Training injuries range from the minor, such as blisters, to the potentially very serious, such as knee and ankle injuries.

(continued on p. 73)

Did You Know That . . .

Sports that qualify as pain-free are swimming, walking, and cross-country skiing, because for the most part they can be done without sharp, sudden movements, severe arching of the back, twisting or rotating the trunk, heavy impact, and unexpected, awkward falls.

1. Overdoing it. Pushing yourself too hard, too long, or too often is probably the leading cause of sports injury. Studies show, for example, that working out more than four times a week in a high-impact activity like running or aerobic dance puts you at significantly higher risk. So does dramatically increasing your workload—whether it's the amount of weight you lift, the speed or distance you cycle, or the number of hours you play tennis.

Five Factors That Put You at Risk

2. Inadequate footwear and equipment. Wearing improper or worn-out shoes places added stress on your hips, knees, ankles, and feet—the sites of up to 90% of all sports injuries. Running shoes, for example, offer virtually no protection from the sideways motions typical of aerobic dance, basketball, and racquet sports. With frequent use, athletic shoes can also lose one-third or more of their shock-absorbing ability in a matter of months.

Poor equipment is another risk factor. Riding a bicycle that is too small or that has its seat set too low, for instance, puts undue stress on the knees; a tennis racquet with too large a grip can strain your forearm.

3. Poor conditioning. Being out-of-shape and having weakened, tight muscles increases your risk of injury when you exercise. Problems can also arise from favoring one sport; this is likely to strengthen certain muscles at the expense of others, leaving tendons and ligaments unbalanced and thus vulnerable. For example, shin splints—a common running injury that causes pain in the front of the lower leg—are often the result of an imbalance between the powerful muscles along the back of the lower leg and the relatively weaker ones in front. Varying your activities is one way to prevent this muscle imbalance. Another precaution is to strengthen the muscle groups you underuse, and stretch all muscles involved in your workout.

4. Improper technique and training. In most activities, stress can result from poor form, whether it's landing on the balls of your feet (instead of your heels) when jogging, using an awkward backhand in tennis, or constantly cycling in the highest gears. Training practices like running on hills or on hard or uneven surfaces also increase risk. It may pay to consult an expert—such as a teaching tennis pro or trainer—if you have recurrent injuries.

5. Ignoring aches and pains. Studies show that starting to exercise before an injury has healed may not only worsen it, but greatly increases the chance of re-injury. Learn to monitor your body for abnormal sensations, and to apply appropriate treatment as early as possible.

Source: *University of California Berkeley Wellness Letter,* March 1990, p. 4.

- *Blisters* are the body's attempt to protect the inner layer of the skin, which is responsible for the regeneration and growth of the skin, from damage caused by excess friction. When excess friction occurs and the inner layer is threatened with damage, the body responds by filling the space between the inner layer and the outer protective layer of the skin with fluid to provide a protective cushion. Blisters can be prevented by wearing two pairs of good quality socks, properly fitting shoes, and plenty of foot powder. When blisters occur, they should be punctured at the edge by a sterile needle, drained, treated with an antiseptic, and bandaged to avoid infection. A bandage, moleskin, or lubricant may be needed to protect the affected area from further damage when resuming activity.

- *Muscle soreness* that appears within 24 to 48 hours after exercise is known as delayed-onset muscle soreness (DOMS). Such soreness is common at the beginning of an exercise program, but it can also result from a change in exercise habits or from excessively hard training sessions. The best prevention is taking the time to ease into any new routine gradually. A thorough **warm-up** and **cool-down**, including light stretching before and after exercise activity, may also be helpful. Massage and warm baths may provide temporary relief from discomfort—but should not be used to treat an acute injury.

- *Stress fractures*, which are more serious than the above-described training injuries, result from repeated trauma to the bone. Stress fractures often affect the weight-bearing bones, like those in the feet and legs. After an injury takes place, applying ice, wearing proper footwear padding or, if necessary, a support, and stopping the activity that caused the trauma can help. However, it is best to try to *prevent* stress fractures by using footwear that dissipates shock forces. As soon as shoe padding wears out, it must be replaced, or the shoe must be discarded. Two of the best tools for preventing stress fractures and other similar injuries are a carefully planned and gradual increase in exercise intensity coupled with adequate rest.

- *Lower back pain*, which occurs in up to 80 percent of the adult population in the United States, is another potentially serious condition that can be caused by exercise. It may result from poor posture, improper lifting techniques, fatigue, poor flexibility, or weak back and abdominal muscles. Preventive measures include careful lifting techniques, improved posture, adequate rest, and appropriate flexibility, muscle strength, and endurance exercises. A full discussion of lower back pain is beyond the scope of this book, but beginning exercisers should

---

Did You Know That . . .

To treat muscle cramps, either ice packs or hot packs on the muscle may help, followed by massage and gradual stretching.

Warm-up: The initial phase of a workout or exercise session whose purpose is to prepare the body for more strenuous activity; typical warm-up activities include slow jogging, light stretching, or a low-intensity "rehearsal" of the activity to follow.

Cool-down: The concluding phase of a workout or exercise session during which the body gradually returns to near pre-exercise conditions; walking until heart rate and respiration return to near normal is an example of a cool-down activity.

be aware that if such pain persists beyond the initial period of training, an examination by a physician is probably in order. The causes of back pain are numerous, ranging from the minor and temporary to the severe and chronic, and only a qualified health-care professional can rule out such serious causes as a severe disk problem.

- *Knee pain* sometimes results from overuse associated with endurance-type training such as running. Other frequent causes are improper or excessively worn footwear or training on uneven surfaces. Elimination of the causal conditions is the best prevention. Rest is the best treatment. If the problem continues, a doctor should be consulted.
- *Ankle injuries* often occur as the result of sharp turning motions or exercising on uneven surfaces. If a sprain occurs, the ankle should be wrapped and treated with ice immediately and examined by a doctor. Strengthening exercises for the muscles around the ankle joint and footwear which provides good ankle support are the best prevention.
- *Shin splints* is a term used to describe a number of injuries involving the shin area of the leg. These injuries are characterized by sharp pains on the front of the tibia, or shin bone. Among the possible causes are a structural problem in the arch of the foot, a tearing away of the shin bone's outer layer, a hairline fracture, or a muscle tear. Rest and ice are the standard treatments. These are sometimes combined with taping the affected area and, perhaps, switching to an alternative form of exercise that minimizes trauma to the leg, such as swimming. Shin injuries are best prevented by using appropriate foot protection, strengthening the surrounding musculature, and avoiding drastic increases in training duration or intensity.
- *Achilles tendon injuries* are often caused by foot abnormalities such as flat feet or high arches, and by failing to provide sufficient time for strengthening of the tendons before engaging in intense activity. The problem can be aggravated by improper footwear or weakness in the muscles that support the foot. Applying ice packs, combined with reduced activity or total rest, is the only treatment for minor cases. Proper footwear and warm-up with adequate stretching are the best preventive measures. A physician should be consulted in the case of any questionable or sustained pain or injury.

R.I.C.E. principle: Rest, ice, compression, and elevation. The purpose of this treatment is to reduce pain, decrease swelling, and limit the amount of inflammation induced by an injury.

The first-aid treatment that is most often recommended for many training injuries is known as the **R.I.C.E. principle** (or RICE for short). The acronym comes from the first letters of the 4

R.I.C.E.

Here are the 4 steps of the R.I.C.E. principle discussed below.

- REST: Complete rest may be required for severe injuries. Other injuries may simply need a modification in mode, impact, frequency, intensity, or duration of exercise.
- ICE: Proper icing technique, particularly in the first 24 to 48 hours after the incident, can effectively reduce pain, swelling, and inflammation. It encourages blood vessels to constrict and slows the conduction of nerve impulses. Cold may be applied in the form of ice packs or chemical cold packs. A favorite approach in sports medicine is to freeze paper cups that are half-filled with water. At the time of use, simply peel off the lip of the cup. The base of the cup provides a handle for ice massage.

- Cold should be applied for no more than 10 to 20 minutes every hour, as greater amounts of time can result in a reflex blood-vessel dilation, which should be avoided.
- COMPRESSION: The application of compression also helps to reduce inflammation and can control bleeding. Common forms of compression include applying pressure to a bleeding wound, and wrapping an injury site with an elastic bandage.
- ELEVATION: Elevating the injured area so that the injury is higher than the heart is another strategy to reduce swelling. It decreases blood flow to and assists in drainage from the injury site.

basic steps—rest, ice, **compression**, and elevation. The purpose of this treatment is to reduce pain, decrease swelling, and limit the amount of inflammation induced by the injury. The R.I.C.E. principle is highly effective in many cases. [8] Because inflammation not only increases pain but may also retard the healing process, the R.I.C.E. procedure is appropriate only as an immediate measure. It should not be used in place of consultation with a qualified sports medicine professional.

Although heat is used by sports medicine professionals to treat certain injuries, the use of heat as a first-aid treatment for injuries is generally not advisable. Heat can actually promote inflammation by dilating blood vessels and increasing blood flow to the site of injury. In particular, heat should not be applied to acute, new injuries.

Hot tubs and jacuzzis are very popular for relaxation, and may provide temporary relief for many muscle aches and stiffness. However, they should not be used immediately after exercise, before the body has had time to cool down and the pulse rate has returned to normal. Use of such appliances under the wrong circumstances can lead to dizziness, abnormal heart rhythms,

Compression: Wrapping an injured area with an elastic bandage or similar device immediately following injury, in an attempt to minimize swelling.

(continued on p. 79)

Treatment of Exercise Injuries

The injuries to muscles, tendons, and joints that can trouble active people are often preventable. . . . Unfortunately, though, no matter how careful people are, exercise injuries will occur. Here's how to deal with some of the more common ones:

When should you see a doctor?

It depends both on the type of injury and, especially, on how serious it is. A severe acute injury (one that occurs suddenly) may indeed require medical attention. Call a doctor if any of the following symptoms persist: stabbing or radiating pain, numbness or tingling, significant swelling, or inability to move the injured body part.

Overuse injuries such as tennis elbow or runner's knee, which are due to the cumulative wear and tear of a repetitive movement, probably won't require a doctor's care. In fact, self-treatment is generally just what the doctor recommends. However, if pain persists for more than 10 days in spite of self-care measures, or if it is severe or is growing worse, consult a doctor.

What's the first thing you should do to treat an injury?

Apply ice. This the most effective, safest, and cheapest form of treatment. With acute injuries such as torn ligaments, muscle strains, and bruises, *start icing as soon as possible.* Even if you're on your way to the doctor, starting to ice the injury right away will help speed recovery. Not only does ice relieve pain, but it also slows blood flow, thereby reducing internal bleeding and swelling. This in turn helps limit tissue damage and hastens the healing process (see box at right).

How should you apply ice? How often?

Although commercial ice packs are available, plain ice is fine: simply put ice cubes or crushed ice in a heavy plastic bag or hot-water bottle, or wrap the ice in a towel.

Apply the ice to the injured area for 10 to 20 minutes, then re-apply it every two waking hours for the next 48 hours. Be sure not to go over the 20-minute limit; longer than that may damage the skin and nerves.

If you start to feel *mild* discomfort when exercising and think it may be the first sign of an overuse injury, such as tendinitis, you may well be able to finish your activity—a set of tennis, for example. But apply ice to the tender areas right after you finish, and re-apply it several times a day for the next 48 hours.

If swelling occurs, which is likely with acute injuries, use ice in conjunction with three other measures that are often referred to as RICE:

> **R**est the injured body part;
> apply **I**ce;
> apply **C**ompression;
> **E**levate the injured extremity above heart level.

Resting not only reduces pain, but also helps prevent aggravating the injury. To apply compression, wrap a towel or an Ace-type elastic bandage around the injury (not so tightly that you cut off circulation). You can often combine ice and compression by holding the ice pack in place with a bandage.

When should you apply heat to an injury?

Traditionally people started applying heat to an injury soon after icing it. But heat actually stimulates blood flow and so increases inflammation. Most sports physicians and trainers now recommend that you stick with ice for at least the first 48 hours after an injury, and only then, *after swelling has subsided,* try heat. At that point, heat may speed up healing, help relieve pain, relax muscles, and reduce joint stiffness.

You can apply either dry heat (using a heating pad or lamp) or moist heat (a hot bath, whirlpool, hot-water bottle, heat pack, or damp towel wrapped around a waterproof heating pad). There's much debate about whether dry or moist heat is best, and for what type of injury, so check with your doctor about which is appropriate for you. If you have a heart condition, for instance, he may tell you to avoid using a hot bath or whirlpool. He will probably also advise against these if you have a fever or infection, or if the injury is bleeding. Also call your doctor if pain or inflammation gets worse after heating an injury.

The key word is "warm," not "hot." Use heating pads on low or medium settings, and keep the water in baths between 98° and 105° F. (The water should feel comfortable when you dip your wrist in.) Apply the heat for 20 to 30 minutes, two or three times a day. You can also use it for 5 to 10 minutes before exercising in order to reduce stiffness.

How injuries heal

Injured tendons, muscles, ligaments, and cartilage (the types of soft tissue involved in most exercise injuries) can take a long time to heal—longer, in fact, than broken bones. The aim of treatment is to assist the natural healing process, which occurs in several stages:

• **Inflammation.** In this initial response to injury, blood vessels in surrounding tissue dilate and release a variety of substances. White blood cells arrive to remove dead tissue and other debris. These and other vascular changes produce heat, swelling, and redness. The subsequent pain and stiffness have the beneficial effect of keeping you from moving and aggravating the injured muscles or other body parts.

• **Regeneration.** After 24 to 48 hours, the body begins replacing injured tissue. Damaged cells are flushed from the area, then capillaries form, allowing a greater flow of oxygen and nutrients into the injury site. Two to three days after the initial damage, strands of collagen—a protein that is the major component of connective tissue—begin forming scar tissue over the damaged areas, a process that lasts two to three weeks.

• **Remodeling.** If you don't move the injured body part at all, the collagen will grow into a puckered, inelastic scar that remains weak and can cause tightness and discomfort—particularly in muscles, which are normally far more elastic than tendons or ligaments. That's why you should gently stretch and strengthen damaged tissue once

the pain subsides. When it recovers properly, the affected muscle or tendon usually regains 80 to 95% of its original strength within three to six months. There will always be at least a slight residual loss in strength.

Injury specialists

Sports medicine is a rapidly growing field. However, there's no board certification for "sports medicine," and so-called "sports doctors" have varied training and specialties. Your family doctor will be able to treat common sprains and strains, but for more severe or complicated injuries he may refer you to one of the following:

Orthopedists are MDs with specialized surgical training. They treat injuries to any part of the musculoskeletal system; some specialize in athletic injuries.

Physical therapists administer techniques to enhance recovery, from massage to rehabilitative exercises. A therapist typically has a degree in physical therapy and is licensed by the state as a registered physical therapist (RPT). You'll need a doctor's referral in most states.

Podiatrists deal with foot and foot-related injuries. Though not MDs, podiatrists receive special training and are licensed by the state.

Sports medicine clinics are likely to include some of the specialists mentioned above. Check with your local medical center to see if it has a sports medicine clinic or department or if there's one in the area.

Should you take pain relievers? Will special anti-inflammatory drugs help?

Taking aspirin or ibuprofen (such as Motrin or Advil) can indeed help ease the pain and reduce inflammation of minor sprains, strains, and tendinitis. However, the other major over-the-counter pain reliever, acetaminophen (such as Tylenol), is less helpful since it has no anti-inflammatory effect.

There are more potent prescription medications, widely recommended by athletic trainers, which can eliminate pain and swelling very quickly in many cases. But these drugs—including cortisone, the strongest of all anti-inflammatory medications—can produce serious side effects. Another potential problem: they can let you ignore the pain, which is a warning sign, and allow you to exercise vigorously, perhaps resulting in permanent damage to the injured tissue. Hence such drugs should be used only under medical supervision and only for brief periods of time.

Should you stop exercising completely—and for how long?

For most overuse injuries, rest a day or two and then try to exercise the affected area at an intensity that doesn't cause pain. You can try to gradually return to your usual workout routine, initially reducing your speed, duration, and/or frequency by at least 25%. Don't work out, though, if persistent pain returns, and don't resume your normal level until you are free of pain both during and after exercise. It's also important to identify the cause of the injury—poor equipment, poor technique, or some other factor—and correct it.

For minor strains and sprains—if you twist your ankle slightly while hiking, for example—staying off the injured part for a day or two is often enough. More serious injuries will require a longer rest period, and you may have to immobilize the injured part, by keeping weight off a wrenched knee, for example, or supporting an injured wrist or elbow in a sling. Check with your doctor.

Unless an injury is severe, however, absolute rest shouldn't exceed 48 hours. Otherwise, muscles may weaken, joints may stiffen, and the scar tissue that forms around the injury may start to tighten. Activity helps prevent this and, by increasing blood flow, also encourages healing.

As soon as the initial pain and swelling of a sprain or other acute injury subside, therefore, you should begin to exercise the injured area *gently*. Do stretching and strengthening exercises that move the affected muscles through their full range of motion. To maintain aerobic fitness, you can substitute another activity that puts less stress on the injured part. If you're a jogger with a sprained ankle, for instance, try cycling or swimming until you recover.

What about those much-advertised liniments?

Liniments and balms are popular, convenient methods for producing a feeling of heat in muscles. But their effect is only superficial—the active ingredients stimulate sensory nerve endings in the skin just enough to produce sensations of heat or cold that may temporarily mask the pain of sore muscles. The massaging action of applying the liniment can increase blood flow and help relax muscles. But since the heating action is only superficial, it does little or nothing to promote healing. **Note:** never put liniment over a wound; and never cover liniment with a heating pad or elastic bandage, since this may cause burning and blistering.

What's the best way to treat muscle soreness that results from "overdoing it"?

Stiff, sore muscles are common in weekend athletes who exercise only occasionally, as well as in frequent exercisers who suddenly increase the intensity of their workouts. Called delayed-onset muscle soreness (DOMS), this type of discomfort—which may start a day or two later and can last a week or more—probably results from microscopic injury to muscle tissue, but appears not to lead to long-term damage.

There is no proven treatment for DOMS. Not exercising for five to seven days can ease the discomfort. However, "active" rest may be better: recent research suggests that relief from DOMS may be achieved by repeating the activity that caused the soreness, but at a much lower intensity.

If DOMS becomes very uncomfortable and you want to take a pain reliever, don't reach for aspirin or ibuprofen. Though these can help you cope with a sprain or strain (as discussed above), new evidence suggests that in the case of DOMS these drugs may interfere with muscle repair and thus prolong the soreness. The problem is that they block the body's production of prostaglandins, substances that help stimulate the repair process. Thus acetaminophen, which has no anti-prostaglandin effect, is probably your best choice for muscle soreness.

Source: *University of California Berkeley Wellness Letter,* May 1990, pp. 4–5.

and blood pressure problems. People with diagnosed heart conditions should avoid using them at any time.

Proper Exercise Gear and Equipment

The use of proper exercise gear and equipment can go a long way toward preventing unnecessary injuries. Appropriate clothing is necessary to compensate for the effects of extreme temperatures,

(continued on p. 81)

FIGURE 4.4
Proper Footwear for Running

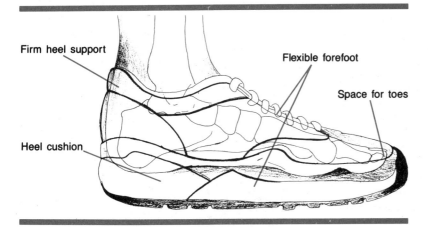

Firm heel support

Flexible forefoot

Space for toes

Heel cushion

Athletic shoes are designed and constructed for specific activities. A well-fitted running shoe should feel snug, but have room in the front for some movement of the toes. A firm heel support will stabilize the foot, and heel cushioning will provide resiliency on impact. A flexible forefoot will enhance the natural flexing of the foot for running.

Who Are the Experts?

What's the best brand of athletic shoes? Which foods promote top sports performance? Where should you buy your new bicycle? When should you start a fitness program? How can you achieve maximum strength and flexibility?

Once you make a commitment to fitness and a healthy lifestyle, you may have a lot of questions about exercise, food, and equipment choices. One of the most important questions you can ask is: Who are the experts to turn to for advice?

When the fitness craze came into full swing in the 1980s, books, magazine articles, television reports, and advertisements bombarded the American public with information. Today, interest in fitness remains high, and people who want to get healthy and stay that way must sort out fitness facts from fiction.

But how? One way to be sure you're getting accurate information is to look for authoritative, objective sources, preferably people with a combination of an academic degree and experience in the field of sports or training, who are not trying to sell you a product.

Fitness has two basic components: nutrition and exercise. Look for experts in either field, or someone with experience in both. One good source of information about proper diet is your family doctor. Another is a registered dietitian. Your local hospital is also a good source. Home economists, family-living teachers, and registered nurses can also offer sound, objective advice.

If you have questions about exercise, start with your health or physical education teacher. Other good authorities are people with a master's or Ph.D. degree in exercise science or exercise physiology and experience with coaching or participation in athletics. Registered athletic trainers also have special expertise in fitness training and injury prevention, as do sports medicine physicians.

Author, Author

Look for the same kind of expertise in books and articles about fitness. Book authors and sources

quoted in magazine articles should have good credentials. Research reports should cite references.

A good way to assess the value of information in a magazine article is to look for a well-qualified advisory board listed in the magazine along with the names of the publisher, editor, and other staff members. (This is usually at the front of a magazine.) Keep in mind that these people may screen articles, but probably don't approve the content of advertising in the magazine.

Advertisers are trying to sell their products. Although consumers are somewhat protected by truth-in-advertising laws, some degree of exaggeration is allowed. Adopt a suspicious attitude, even when claims seem to be supported by scientific research. You'll be better off if you look for results of research reported in reputable scientific journals.

Professional associations and organizations that promote good health and nutrition information are also good authorities. Two organizations with a good reputation are the American College of Sports Medicine and the American Alliance for Health, Physical Education, Recreation, and Dance. Ask your health or physical education teacher to help you consult their journals for specific information on a subject.

Groups like the American Heart Association, the American Dietetic Association, and organizations that oversee individual sports, such as U.S. Swimming, are also good places to seek objective information. So is the President's Council on Physical Fitness and Sports, which offers guidelines for fitness and exercise.

Buyer Beware

Asking for sound credentials and objectivity are just two ways of being an informed fitness consumer. You can also learn to spot telltale signs of inaccurate information. Beware of articles that stress fads or emphasize one type of food, product, or program. Everyone has different fitness goals, so authorities should offer a variety of ways to achieve them.

Shy away from articles or people who advise you to take steroids or supplements such as powdered proteins to enhance your health. These products have not been proven advantageous, and they can be extremely dangerous. Anyone who recommends such substances does not have your best interest in mind.

Avoid articles about diets that claim fast weight loss in short periods of time. Experts agree the best way to lose weight is through life-style changes that emphasize balanced nutrition and regular exercise.

If you are considering an investment in fitness equipment such as a treadmill, stationary bike, stair climber, or cross-country skiing machine, you'll need the same consumer skills you use for other major purchases. This home equipment comes in a wide variety of quality and price ranges.

Do Your Homework

Before shopping, do your homework. Consult consumer magazines like *Consumer Reports* and special interest magazines that run reviews of various equipment. You would be wise to shop in person. Mail order equipment may seem like a bargain, but even if the company offers a money-back guarantee, you give up the chance to try out the equipment before you buy.

Choose a reputable store that offers a variety of manufacturers' products and whose sales clerks are knowledgeable and willing to take time to help you. Check with the Better Business Bureau to see if anyone has complained about the store's business practices. Compare quality and price, and ask how features of different models will meet your fitness needs.

Don't buy any equipment until you've had a chance to try it, either in the store or at a fitness club. If the store won't let you use their display equipment and can't suggest a place you can try it, shop somewhere else.

Shop around anyway. Always get a second opinion—or more. Compare prices, features, and sales pitches. Be sure to ask where you can get parts for the equipment if it needs repair. Ask competitors what they think of each other's products. Sales representatives may make the same recommendations, or they may vary widely. Add what they say to information you've acquired from independent media to form your opinion.

Ultimately, decisions about your fitness program are yours. For best results, screen information carefully. Expert opinions based on scientific research are available, but you'll probably have to sort through some less reliable information, too. Pay attention to the credentials and experience of authors and people who claim to be in the know before adopting their advice.

Source: Mary Lane-Kamberg, *Current Health 2* (November 1990), pp. 26–27.

as discussed earlier. Safety gear, such as helmets for cycling and lights and reflective materials for training in the dark, should be used whenever it is appropriate.

The importance of footwear is often overlooked. Use footwear that is designed for the particular exercise activity you've chosen—running shoes for running, tennis shoes for tennis, etc. It is also crucial to replace shoes when they begin to wear out. Worn shoes have inadequate shock absorption, are often unstable, and have uneven sole wear. Training in worn shoes can lead to injury and loss of precious training time. The cost of good-quality athletic footwear may seem prohibitive; but, when weighed against the risk of injury, the price may indeed be justified.

EXERCISING SAFELY

High-top shoes may protect against ankle sprains by stabilizing the ankles and preventing a rollover, or inversion, onto the side of the foot.

All of the above potential sources of injury risk are preventable in most cases with the use of common sense. As a first step, set realistic, attainable exercise goals, based on sound knowledge and advice. Tailor a well-structured training program—if possible, with the assistance of a trusted exercise professional—to your needs. And stick to that program; the physical progress you make will be of great help in injury prevention.

Finally, be patient. Improvements in fitness require a sufficient training workload, adequate time for recovery between sessions, a sensible progression in intensity and duration, and, above all, time. 𝕎

Types of Exercise Programs

A WELL-DESIGNED EXERCISE program should be tailored to meet an individual's specific goals and needs. A comprehensive fitness program, for example, might consist of several "subprograms," each of which is designed to improve a specific type of fitness—cardiovascular or aerobic fitness, muscular strength and endurance, and flexibility—and each of which receives roughly equal emphasis. Alternatively, a program whose primary focus is aerobic fitness might concentrate on activities designed to improve cardiovascular conditioning and give less attention to activities designed to enhance other types of fitness such as muscular strength. You might choose, for example, to bicycle 3 times a week—on Monday, Wednesday, and Friday—to improve your cardiovascular fitness while training with weights on Tuesdays and Thursdays.

In short, while most exercise programs will include at least a sampling of activities designed to enhance all of the major fitness components, the relative emphasis placed on each of these components—cardiovascular fitness, muscular strength and endurance, and flexibility—will be dictated by the desired outcome.

On the other hand, while individual exercise programs will vary in terms of emphasis, certain features are common to all well-designed programs. No matter what its goals, for example, any exercise program should allow enough time for proper warm-up and cool-down in addition to the activities that comprise the main portion of each **exercise session**.

Exercise session: The time period within which a complete set of exercises is completed; each session consists of 3 phases—warm-up, main stimulus activity, and cool-down.

Did You Know That . . .

Water exercise, also known as aquaerobics, a fitness alternative to swimming, includes sit-ups, leg lifts, and jumping jacks. Warm up by "water walking" and "water jogging."

COMPONENTS OF AN EXERCISE SESSION

Each session of a well-designed exercise program will be divided into 3 distinct phases—the warm-up phase, the main stimulus activity, and the cool-down phase. Because so much emphasis is often placed on the second of these phases, the main stimulus activity, the warm-up and cool-down are sometimes neglected. However, they are just as important as the main stimulus activity, and should be just as carefully designed in light of the overall program goals and the specific requirements of the exercise session involved.

Warm-Up

Every workout session, particularly if it demands a high level of intensity, should include one or more warm-up activities. In general, the warm-up phase consists of two stages. First is the *general warm-up,* which prepares the cardiovascular system for more strenuous physical activity. Typical activities for this stage include walking, slow jogging, or cycling. Second come the *specific warm-up* exercises that are designed to prepare the particular muscle groups that will be most active during the main stimulus activity. Typical activities during this stage of the warm-up include practice serves (in tennis) or low-resistance weight exercises. The general warm-up stage of a weight training program, for example, might consist of 10 minutes of stationary cycling and some light stretching. This might be followed by a "rehearsal" for a particular lift such as the bench press, involving the use of much lighter weights than will be used during the main stimulus activity.

The duration and intensity chosen for the warm-up depend on several factors. One is the individual's fitness level. Unfit people need a relatively less intense, more gradual, and longer warm-up than those who are more fit. A second factor is environmental conditions. For instance, a longer warm-up may be needed in cold weather. The third factor is the intensity of the main stimulus activity. An intense activity like sprinting, for example, requires a longer warm-up than that for a mild activity like walking.

A typical warm-up for a moderate cardiovascular activity might begin with a general warm-up of approximately 5 minutes, consisting of movements that involve as many muscle groups as possible (such as walking). These should begin at a very low intensity and gradually increase, so that the metabolic and heart

FIGURE 5.1
Whole Body Movement

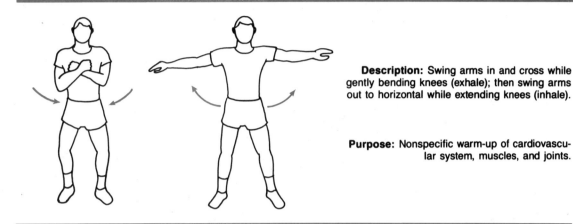

Description: Swing arms in and cross while gently bending knees (exhale); then swing arms out to horizontal while extending knees (inhale).

Purpose: Nonspecific warm-up of cardiovascular system, muscles, and joints.

The movement shown here is an example of an activity that, in combination with other such activities, is an appropriate general warm-up or cool-down activity for almost any form of exercise. A slow, easy walk is a nice substitute.

rates and the body's core temperature also increase gradually. This initial period might be followed by 5 minutes of stretching exercises that take the joints and muscles through the ranges of motion required for the actual workout. Properly done, this will prepare the joints and muscles for the main stimulus activity.

Main Stimulus Activity

The main stimulus activity is the primary—or fitness training—portion of the exercise session. This is the phase in which the activity or activities whose purpose is to improve a specific fitness component occur. The length of this phase and the amount of effort required translate into 2 key variables, duration and intensity. This phase of the exercise session may be further broken down into subcomponents consisting of different individual activities, each of which has a specific purpose. Some of the many possible types of activities that typically comprise this phase are discussed in the remainder of this chapter.

Cool-Down

The cool-down phase is a critical component of every exercise session. Its purpose is to allow for a gradual return of the heart

FIGURE 5.2
Side Trunk Stretches

Description: While keeping knees slightly bent, abdominal muscles tucked in, and right arm reaching above head, gently lean to the left side while supporting the left hand on the knee. Reverse and repeat 8 times.

Purpose: To warm up the muscles and joints associated with the trunk.

Like the whole body movement exercise shown on the preceding page, the activity shown here is an appropriate general warm-up or cool-down activity for almost any form of exercise.

and metabolic rates to their prestimulus level. During an activity such as running, for example, the heart is pumping blood to the working leg muscles at a high rate. Similarly, the repeated contraction of those muscles helps return blood to the heart, thus assisting the circulatory process. Abruptly halting this activity eliminates the assist provided by the leg muscles, and may lead to an abrupt drop in blood pressure (hypotension) caused by the pooling of blood in the legs. This may in turn result in dizziness or even fainting.

For training activities that substantially increase the heart rate, like running and cycling, a cool-down that begins with a "dynamic" portion of 5 to 10 minutes is often appropriate. This may consist of very mild cardiovascular activity, such as very slow jogging, walking, or riding a stationary bicycle until the heart rate significantly declines. Although there is no specific heart rate that applies to all situations, many professionals recommend a decline to 120 beats per minute as an appropriate target figure for most adults.

Once this level has been reached, an additional 5 to 10 minutes can be spent doing stretching or floor exercises to finish the cool-down. However, floor exercises should not begin until after the dynamic portion of the cool-down is complete, as a sudden change in posture while the heart rate is still high can be stressful to the cardiovascular system.

A PROGRAM FOR CARDIOVASCULAR FITNESS

Typically, the activities that are employed in cardiovascular training are rhythmic and aerobic in nature, use large muscle groups and a large portion of the body's muscle mass, and place a substantial demand on the cardiovascular system to supply oxygen to working muscles. [1] (See chapter 2.) Many activities fit this description, including walking, running, cycling, swimming, aerobic dancing, bench stepping, and cross-country skiing.

There are two basic, complementary approaches to cardiovascular training: endurance training and interval training. In endurance training, exercise is performed continuously, over longer periods of time, at a relatively constant level of intensity.

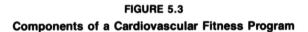

FIGURE 5.3
Components of a Cardiovascular Fitness Program

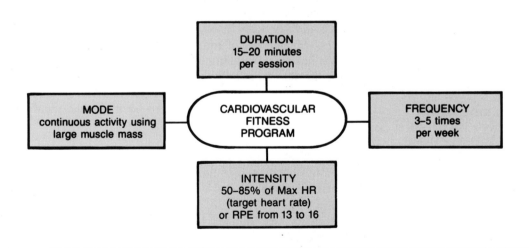

Duration, frequency, intensity, and mode are the four components of a cardiovascular fitness program that can be varied to achieve optimum results.

Did You Know That . . .

A U.S. Preventive Services Task Force survey concluded that the greatest benefits from exercise come at the earliest and least strenuous levels—and grow incrementally smaller as workout intensity increases.

In what is known as **interval training**, shorter repetitions of higher-intensity exercise are interspersed with lower-intensity—but still active—"recovery periods." [2]

Both endurance training and interval training increase VO_2 max and thus improve cardiovascular fitness. Interval training may be more effective in this area. However, endurance training appears to do more for skeletal muscles than even high-intensity interval training, and is likely to be more tolerable to previously untrained subjects because it involves somewhat lower-intensity workouts than interval training. Early in any cardiovascular training program, however, it is certainly acceptable to intersperse rest and activity at low intensity in a manner patterned after the interval model.

Frequency, Intensity, and Duration

Some general guidelines for frequency, intensity, and duration of cardiovascular training have been established by the American College of Sports Medicine (ACSM). [3] These guidelines were developed specifically to improve cardiovascular fitness, and they vary in accordance with the fitness level and health status of the participant.

The ACSM guidelines for apparently healthy individuals are as follows:

- An initial minimum *frequency* of 3 times per week, progressing, as fitness improves, to as many as 5 times per week.
- An initial *intensity* equal to one of the following: (a) 55 to 90 percent of maximum heart rate; (b) 40 to 85 percent of VO_2 max; (c) 50 to 85 percent of **maximum heart rate reserve**; or (d) a perceived exertion rating of somewhat hard to hard (from 13 to 16 on the 20-point RPE scale; see p. 91).
- An initial *duration* of 15 to 20 minutes of activity at the target heart rate per exercise session, to be increased gradually as fitness increases.

Interval training: Alternating repetitions of higher-intensity exercise interspersed with lower-intensity but still active "recovery periods." Increases VO_2 max and thus cardiovascular fitness.

Maximum heart rate reserve: The range between an individual's resting and maximum heart rates; the target heart rate for any given individual and set of exercises will fall within this range.

Since these guidelines are quite broad, the beginner should start at the lower end of these recommended ranges and gradually increase the frequency, intensity, and duration of his or her workouts as is appropriate. It should be noted too that duration and intensity are related to one another, and that the same results can often be obtained from various combinations of the two, for example, an increase in duration accompanied by a proportional decrease in intensity. There is, therefore, usually more than one formula that will produce the desired results.

An appropriate level of intensity is one of the most important factors in any successful training program. (As noted in chapter 4, it is also a major factor in promoting exercise safety.) The 3 most commonly used indicators of intensity are heart rate, perceived exertion, and percentage of VO_2 max. The first two are the easiest and simplest methods for most exercisers. (Measuring percentage of VO_2 max requires equipment that is unavailable in most exercise settings.)

Measurement of Heart Rate   The most practical and versatile method for monitoring exercise intensity is target heart rate, which is calculated as a percentage of the maximum heart rate reserve. The target heart rate (target HR) can be determined using the following formula. Here, we use the example of target HR at 60 percent of maximum heart rate reserve:

Target HR = (maximum HR − resting HR) × 0.60 + resting HR

Maximum heart rate (maximum HR), in beats per minute, is estimated by subtracting the subject's age from 220.

Resting heart rate (resting HR), in beats per minute, is preferably taken just after awakening in the morning and before rising from bed.

A target HR range between 50 and 85 percent of maximum heart rate reserve is often suggested. [4] However, for most people, particularly in the early stages of a training program, it is probably more appropriate to use a slightly more conservative range of 50 to 75 percent. (See Figure 5.4 on page 90.) Previously sedentary and obese participants should begin exercising at the lower end of this range. In some cases, an even lower intensity may be prudent, depending on the advice of a doctor and the individual's tolerance for exercise.

Since it is impractical to stop for a full minute during an exercise session to measure your heart rate, a 10-second count is generally recommended. To do this, stop briefly, locate the appropriate place on your wrist (radial pulse) or neck (carotid pulse), and count your pulse for an interval of 10 full seconds, counting your first pulse as zero.

Consider, for example, a 20-year-old woman with a resting heart rate of 65 beats per minute whose maximum heart rate is 200 (220 minus her age). If she wants to exercise at an intensity level of 60 to 70 percent, her target heart rate zone will be between 146 and 160 beats per minute. This in turn corresponds to a 10-second count of between 24 and 27. In her case, a 10-second

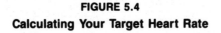

FIGURE 5.4
Calculating Your Target Heart Rate

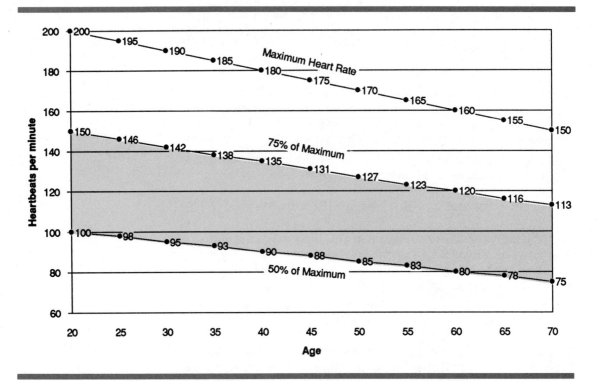

To find your target heart rate, locate your age at the bottom of the chart. The lower edge of the shaded area above your age is the lower limit of your target zone. The upper edge of the shaded area is the upper limit.

heart rate below 24 indicates a need to increase intensity, while a 10-second heart rate above 27 will indicate a need to slow down.

There are two appropriate places to take a person's pulse: at the radial artery at the wrist or at one of the carotid arteries in the neck. In taking one's pulse, the fingertips should be used rather than the thumb, because the fingertips are more sensitive. *Note:* Only gentle pressure at one side of the neck should be used when taking the pulse at the carotid artery. Too great an application of pressure can alter the heart rate and result in miscalculation.

Perceived Exertion Another practical method for assessing exercise intensity is the Rating of Perceived Exertion (RPE) scale.

[5] This 20-point system (see Table 5.1) relies on a person's *subjective* feeling of exertion. The RPE has been shown to correlate quite well with cardiovascular and metabolic indicators such as heart rate and percentage of VO_2 max during exercise of constant intensity. For example, a woman who rates her exertion as a "13," or "somewhat hard," during a session of bench stepping is likely to be exercising at about 60 percent of her maximum heart rate reserve.

The RPE scale is used extensively in medical and health clinics during **graded exercise testing**. It is also used with individuals for whom heart rate monitoring is unreliable (for example, those on medication for a heart condition or blood pressure). The RPE is also recommended for people who have difficulty finding and monitoring their pulses.

Table 5.1 The Rating of Perceived Exertion (RPE) Scale

6	
7	Very, Very Light
8	
9	Very Light
10	
11	Fairly Light
12	
13	Somewhat Hard
14	
15	Hard
16	
17	Very Hard
18	
19	Very, Very Hard
20	

The Rating of Perceived Exertion Scale is a method of evaluating exercise intensity that relies on the individual's perception of how hard he or she is working. A rating from 13 to 16 has been found to correlate well with target heart rate.

Graded exercise testing: Testing to determine exercise capacity during continuous cardiovascular work; usually performed on a treadmill or stationary cycle, it involves gradually increasing the amount of work performed until the individual reaches his or her VO_2 max; sometimes abbreviated as GXT.

Can You Get a
"Second Wind"?

As anyone who has exercised knows, you are likely to feel particularly uncomfortable for the first few minutes after you begin. This can be explained, at least in part, by an imbalance between the amount of oxygen required by the working muscles and the ability of the cardiovascular system to deliver it. However, as time goes on, the heart rate increases and the arteries and capillaries that control the flow of blood to the muscles gradually open. As this occurs, the amount of blood pumped per heartbeat also increases until a point of equilibrium is reached. It has been suggested that achieving this "steady state" corresponds with the sensation of "getting a second wind." There is, however, as yet little experimental evidence to support this belief.

For most persons and activities, an RPE of from 13 ("somewhat hard") to 16 ("hard") during exercise is recommended. This may not apply to people with particular health problems or those unaccustomed to exercise, however, as these guidelines are designed for persons of "average" health. It is also possible that people who are normally active may find this level of intensity insufficient for promoting a further improvement in fitness.

Progression

As fitness improves, exercise sessions that were previously perceived as strenuous become easier and easier. Eventually they will no longer provide the stimulus necessary for continued improvement in fitness. Further improvement in cardiovascular fitness will then require an increase in frequency, intensity, and duration of the exercise, or some combination thereof. Of these variables, the most important is intensity, for increased intensity is strongly associated with improvements in VO_2 max.

The rate at which fitness improves is dependent on many factors, including age, heredity, prior level of fitness, and nutrition. Each individual progresses at his or her own rate. Furthermore, there is no "ideal" or "average" manner of improvement in fitness that is appropriate for everyone.

The way in which a training program progresses is also largely dependent on one's personal fitness goals. A person whose goal is weight loss, and who has been relatively sedentary prior to starting an exercise program, should generally aim to increase frequency and duration more than intensity. While increasing intensity will also increase caloric expenditure, it is likely to prove difficult for many overweight people. Thus, a better strategy for such individuals often involves gradual increases in frequency and duration with an emphasis on low-impact cardiovascular exercises such as brisk walking, cycling, or low-impact aerobic dance which does not place too much stress on joints and bones—a critical concern for obese people. Properly designed, such a program can and will result in an increase in caloric consumption sufficient to stimulate weight loss.

A person who aims to improve his or her aerobic fitness or performance time in an activity like running will want to emphasize increases in intensity to a greater extent than increases in frequency and duration. For example, someone who wants to improve his time in a 10-kilometer race must first be sure he can complete this distance comfortably at a moderate pace (level of intensity). Once this has been accomplished, gradual increases in intensity (pace) will produce the desired training effect, a better race time. However, this strategy may not be tolerated by some people, particularly those who have just begun a program or those who have medical problems. An alternative strategy is to concentrate on increasing the frequency and duration of the training sessions.

Once someone has reached a training goal, he or she will usually be put on a maintenance plan. The amount of training required to maintain a given level of fitness appears to be less than the amount required to reach that level. However, maintaining a given fitness level also appears to require the same degree of intensity, though frequency can be reduced. Furthermore, completely stopping exercise results in fairly rapid deconditioning, so that the measurable indicators of cardiovascular fitness may return to their pretraining levels in as little as 8 to 10 weeks. [6]

A PROGRAM FOR MUSCULAR STRENGTH AND ENDURANCE

As discussed in chapter 2, there are two components to muscular fitness: strength and endurance. Muscular strength is the ability of a muscle or group of muscles to exert a maximal amount of force. Endurance is the ability of a muscle to maintain a specific level of force over time.

Did You Know That . . .

Eating sugar during exercise can cause drowsiness, perhaps because it leads to higher levels of serotonin in the brain, which can act as a sedative.

Did You Know That . . .

Interval circuit training typically refers to exercise sessions in which alternating aerobic and resistance activities of 30 seconds to several minutes each are performed with little or no rest in between.

FIGURE 5.5
The Strength/Endurance Continuum

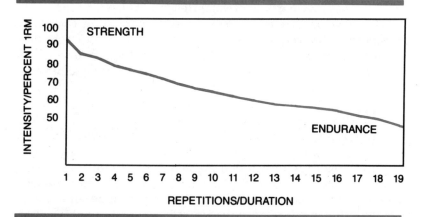

Muscular strength and endurance training exist on a continuum and are dependent upon the variables of intensity and duration. Strength training is characterized by higher intensities and fewer repetitions, while endurance requires lower intensities and greater repetitions.

These 2 components of muscular fitness exist on a continuum and are interdependent. (See Figure 5.5.) Therefore, training programs designed to improve one of these components usually will result in some improvement of the other.

Developing a Personal Weight-Training Program

In designing a weight-training program, there are 3 basic decisions to be made:

- The mode of training and types of exercises, the basic choices being among machines and **free weights**, isotonic and isokinetic training, and Olympic-style weight lifting or power lifting.
- The level of intensity—the amount of weight to use for each exercise; also described as the amount of *resistance*.
- The number of exercise sets and the number of repetitions for each exercise—the overall *volume* of the program.

Free weights: Weights such as dumbbells and barbells that are unattached to any larger piece of apparatus and are used in weight lifting.

Although variations do exist, training programs that emphasize muscular strength usually incorporate higher weight loads and fewer repetitions. Training programs that emphasize muscular endurance use lower weight loads and more repetitions.

(continued on p. 96)

Starting Small With Weights

At first, weight training for the beginner might seem intimidating, whether you are using barbells, known as free weights, or the machines found in health clubs that seem reminiscent of medieval instruments of torture. The people working out are so intense—grunting, groaning and straining, their faces contorted in massive exertion and concentration. Everyone goes around expelling breath in great noisy gasps.

Who needs this, you might ask?

The short answer is that if you are merely interested in the cardiovascular fitness and protection against heart disease that aerobic workouts provide, you can skip weight training with a clear conscience. It does little for aerobic fitness.

On the other hand, once you have begun to seriously put aside a sedentary lifestyle and get aerobically fit, a new awareness of your body usually begins to emerge. You may never intend to carry a baby elephant up the stairs, but if you are muscularly fit, a weekend spent helping a friend move to a new apartment or a day devoted to cleaning out the basement won't be nearly as tiring. Most important, muscular fitness protects against injury while you pursue aerobic fitness through running, racquet sports, aerobic dancing or cycling.

Weight training can be done at home and need not be expensive. . . . Strive for simplicity at first and avoid purchasing weight training benches and other equipment until you know you will stick with weight training. The initial cost should be around $100.

Before beginning, take special note of any areas where you have muscles, tendons or joints that have been prone to injury. Avoid any beginning routines that might put stress on these areas. Remember also that all the warnings issued to fitness beginners about not overdoing apply here, too. A barbell with just 10 pounds of weights on it might seem ridiculously easy to heft above your head, providing a temptation to pile on 20 pounds more and lift away. Don't do it. Instead, begin cautiously. If the weight you choose seems far too easy, it's probably just about right.

The foundation of weight training is putting a muscle under a heavy load and slowly contracting and then relaxing it. Typically, this movement is repeated 8 to 12 times in a training session and then the weight increased by $2^1/2$ to 10 pounds in future sessions when you have grown accustomed to the first weight. The lifting itself should be done slowly and smoothly.

To avoid injury, it is important not to increase the weights at too rapid a pace. Instead, as you progress increase the number of times you perform a movement and then increase the weight, dropping back to a lower number of repetitions with the new weight and working up again.

There are dozens of different routines you can perform with a set of free weights and about as many books on the subject as there are routines. But the neophyte can begin with three simple movements.

Clean and Press: This is performed with the barbell and strengthens a variety of muscles throughout the body. Beginners should use a light weight, perhaps no more than 10 percent of body weight. [Ed. note: In order to minimize injury risk, the clean and press, and other exercises that involve lifting weights over the head, should be attempted only with supervision.]

With the barbell on the floor, squat down slightly and grasp it with the palms facing the floor. Lift the barbell to waist height, straightening the legs and back and being careful to do most of the lifting with the legs. Continue raising the barbell to neck height and then lift it upward high above your head, fully extending the arms. Pause a second and then lower it slowly, stopping at the waist, rather than setting it on the floor. Perform subsequent repetitions beginning at the waist.

Squat: The squat uses the barbell and involves all lower extremity muscles. Begin with weights similar to the clean and press.

Grasp the barbell and lift it to waist height in the same manner as the clean and press. Raise the barbell above your head slightly, move it backward and then lower it so that the bar rests on your shoulders and the back of your neck. Some people place a folded towel on the back of the neck for comfort.

Holding the barbell in this position, slowly squat down, but never so much that the angle at the knee becomes less than 90 degrees, and then return to a fully upright position. In fact, most beginners will want to squat much less than 90 degrees at first, both because of the challenge to leg muscles and because of fear of injuring the knee.

Some people do this movement while straddling a bench about 18 inches high and come down only far enough so that the buttocks touch the bench, so as to further reduce the chance of knee injury.

Biceps Curls: Use a dumbbell with weights set at 7$^{1}/_{2}$ percent of body weight. Sit on a bench and hold the dumbbell in one hand with the palm facing upward and the elbow resting on your knee. While keeping the elbow in place on your knee, raise the dumbbell up to your shoulder, bending the arm at the elbow. The movement should be done only with the arm, using the biceps to raise the dumbbell while keeping the rest of the body still. Repeat with the other arm.

This routine, performed three times a week with steadily increasing weights, will produce impressive results in six to eight weeks.

For those interested in muscle strengthening, one of the great advantages of belonging to a health club is the wide variety of machines avail-able that essentially mimic free-weight routines. But the weights on the machines are easily changed, and various machines using sophisticated systems of cams, cables, compressed air and computer controls can smooth out the movements and more precisely match weights to your strength at the moment.

Manufacturing and selling the machines is a highly competitive industry, and claims about the capabilities of one company's machines are sometimes exaggerated. You need merely remember that your goal is to contract and relax a specific muscle slowly and smoothly under a load, gradually increasing the repetitions and then, later, moving to higher loads. Try out a machine and see if it does that before using it.

Do not attempt to construct a muscle strengthening routine at a health club without seeking help from informed club personnel.

As with free weights, begin with light settings on the machines. It might seem relatively easy to move the machine, but if the weights are too heavy, you will rue the day you ever sat down in the contraption.

There is also a tendency at a club to feel you haven't really worked out unless you have used all the machines. Resist this. Pick out two or three machines that challenge both upper body and lower body muscles and focus for several weeks on their use. Then branch out to some of the specialized devices.

Source: William Stockton, *New York Times* (13 February 1989), p. C-14.

There are many possible effective formats for a strength-oriented training program. One typical format calls for 4 to 6 sets of each exercise using weights greater than 75 percent of the individual's 1 repetition maximum (1RM), with each set consisting of 4 to 6 repetitions. However, this is not an appropriate format for a beginner, who should start with a lighter resistance. As a general rule, someone beginning a strength lifting program should use loads that do not exceed the weight he or she is capable of handling for about 10 repetitions with perfect form. Further, untrained individuals should plan on an adaptation period of at least 2 weeks before increasing the level of resistance above their initial levels. [7]

Practicing proper lifting technique is essential. This allows the exercise to stimulate the muscle through its full range of motion. It also minimizes muscle soreness, a primary cause of early dropout from any program. If proper form cannot be maintained throughout the set, the chosen weight is probably too high.

Because improper weight training can result in injury, advice should be sought if possible from a trained exercise professional when developing a weight-training program. In fact, this is good advice with respect to virtually any sort of exercise program, since there are invariably some risks associated with any type of training. (See, for example, "Exercise Survival Guide" on pages 99–102.)

If a trained professional is unavailable, information can also be obtained from books, periodicals, and other materials. In any case, an appropriate choice of exercises and proper technique is essential to the success of any weight-training program. Observing a few basic principles and seeking advice whenever in doubt can help ensure that weight training remains a safe and enjoyable activity.

Choice of Exercises

Weight-training programs for beginning weight lifters should emphasize safety and balanced development of all the major muscle groups. A program of this type might include the following 9 types of exercises: squats, leg extensions, leg curls, calf raises, bench presses, behind-the-neck presses, the bent row, biceps curls, and triceps presses. (See Figure 5.6 on pages 104–105). Most of these can be performed either with free weights (often called dumbbells or barbells) or machines (such as Nautilus or Universal machines) designed to exercise specific muscle groups. It should also include exercises designed to train the abdominal and lower back muscles. Three sets of 30 abdominal curl-ups and 3 sets of 10 back extensions are suggested.

The order of the workout is important: compound (multijoint) exercises for each region should be performed prior to exercises that involve individual muscles. For instance, squats should be performed before leg extensions. This is because exercises involving the large muscle groups (compound exercises) have the greatest impact on strength. If exercises involving the smaller muscles are done first, this may limit the amount of resistance that can be managed subsequently, thus limiting strength improvement.

(continued on p. 103)

Table 5.2 Weight Training Exercises for Specific Body Regions

Compound lower extremity	Squat Lunge Leg press
Front of thigh	Leg extension
Back of thigh	Leg curl
Calves	Calf raise (standing) Calf press (seated)
Chest	Bench press Incline bench press Chest fly Pec deck
Upper back	Chin-up Lat pull Seated row Bent row
Shoulders	Behind-the-neck press Military press Upright row Lateral dumbbell raise Shrug Parallel bar dip
Arms	Biceps curl Preacher curl Supine triceps extension Seated French press Triceps press at lat station
Abdomen	Abdominal curl-up Crunch Oblique abdominal curl
Low back	Back extension Good morning Opposing limb lift

Different types of exercises stimulate different muscle groups. Shown here are some of the various types of exercises that may be used to train specific sets of muscles.

Exercise Survival Guide

Unlike most machines, the human body improves with regular use—thus exercise can make your cardiovascular system more efficient and your muscles stronger and more limber. But not all exercises performed in classes or in videotaped workouts are good for you. Some are just bad; others are hazardous because they are so often performed incorrectly. And even good exercises can be risky if you overdo them, especially if you're out of shape, have muscle or joint problems, or simply haven't warmed up. That shouldn't scare you off exercise. But it should tell you that you can't just walk into a fitness class or turn on an exercise tape, turn off your mind, and follow orders.

To help you take an active role in selecting exercises and deciding how to do them, here's a list of some of the most commonly done high-risk exercises, along with safer alternatives. The general categories of problems are: overflexing a joint (such as the knee or elbow), overarching the back or neck, sudden twisting or flexing, bouncing while stretching, excessive jumping or hopping, rapid swinging of arms or legs, and poor body alignment.

DON'TS AND DO'S

Straight-leg sit-ups arch the lower back and place excessive stress on it. Also, there's no need to sit up fully, since the abdominal muscles work only during the first part of the movement. After that the hip flexor muscles take over, and the shift to these muscles can pull the hip out of alignment and further arch the back.

Bent-leg sit-ups, also called crunches, are the safest, most effective way to strengthen abdominal muscles. Keep your knees bent and come up only 30° to 45°. Always keep your lower back pressed into the ground to prevent arching. To prevent neck strain, cross your arms over your chest or cross them behind your head so that each hand rests on the opposite shoulder.

Alternating bent-leg sit-ups. By pumping your legs and holding one straight out, you put an asymmetric pull on the pelvis, which can strain the lower back. Also, in your effort to keep both legs off the floor, you may arch your back.

Knee rolls strengthen your oblique abdominal muscles more safely. Lie on your back with your knees up toward your chest and arms out flat at shoulder level. Slowly lower your knees to the right side, trying to keep your lower back on the floor; hold for a few seconds. Slowly return to starting position and lower knees to the left. Hold, then repeat.

Locked-knee toe touches can overstress the back, knees, and hamstring muscles, especially when done quickly with a bouncing movement.

Bent-knee hang downs call for rolling down slowly with your knees slightly bent and abdominal muscles tight until you feel your hamstring and back muscles start to stretch. Hang over for 10 to 20 seconds. Don't use force, don't try to reach the floor, and don't bounce.

Double leg lifts can strain your lower back since raising both legs causes your back to arch. Leg scissors present similar risks.

Raised-leg crunches are a safe way to strengthen abdominal muscles. Keep one leg bent with the foot on the floor; raise the other leg straight up. Raise your upper back and reach toward the lifted ankle.

Yoga plow can compress disks in your neck area. A shoulder stand (or bicycling position in which you rest on your shoulders and upper back) can do similar damage.

Fold-up stretch is a safer way to stretch your upper and lower back. Just sit back on your heels and press your chest to your thighs, reaching forward with your hands.

360° head rolls, in which you vigorously roll your head or bend your head back forcefully, may injure the disks in your neck.

Side neck stretches—use the weight of your hand to pull your head gently to the side and then forward. Also pull it diagonally.

Arched push-ups are sloppy push-ups in which you lower your hips and pelvis to the floor. Like any exercise that arches the back, these can injure the disks in the lower spine. And they do little for arm and shoulder muscles.

Straight-back push-ups give your shoulders and arms the maximum workout without straining your back. Hold your torso in a straight line and slowly lower your chest to the ground by bending your arms at the elbow.

Full squats, like deep knee bends or squat thrusts, greatly increase stress on the knees.

Partial squats strengthen the muscles on the front of your thigh. Squat no more than one-quarter way down: hold on to the wall for support as you extend one leg forward.

Donkey kicks, in which you rapidly lift your leg as high as possible while on all fours, cause the back to arch and also contort the shoulders and neck.

Rear thigh lifts safely work your buttock muscles. Bring your thigh only parallel to your torso. Keep your back straight, and move your leg in a slow, controlled manner.

Swan stretch—lying on your stomach and lifting your chest and legs puts your back in jeopardy.

Prone arm/leg raises strengthen back muscles safely. Lie face down with one or two pillows under your stomach and your arms resting in front of you. Raise your right arm and left leg 4 to 6 inches for 5 seconds. Alternate sides.

EIGHT EXERCISE TIPS

1. Beware of any instructor who says that exercise must hurt (or "burn") to do any good. Exercise should require some effort, but pain is a warning sign you are foolish to ignore. If you have continuing pain during an exercise, stop and don't do it again unless you can do so painlessly.

2. Control all of your movements—if you can't, slow down. Rapid, jerky movement can set the stage for injury. Flailing your arms or legs can overstress joints. Instead, as you move your limbs, keep the muscles in them contracted and move them as if you're pushing against some resistance—for instance, squeezing a beach ball or pushing a weight.

3. Work at your own pace and level of exertion. The pace of many exercise classes is too fast for the average participant. Don't feel constrained to do any set number of repetitions. You don't have to keep up with the instructor or other exercisers or the beat of the music. If a class includes an exercise that is bad or too difficult for you, substitute another.

4. Always watch your posture while exercising: keep your back aligned (abdominal muscles contracted, buttocks tucked in, and knees slightly bent). This is particularly important when jumping or reaching overhead.

5. Don't bounce while stretching. This is called "ballistic" stretching, in which you stretch to your limit and perform quick, pulsing movements. This actually shortens muscles and increases the chance of muscle tears and soreness. Instead, do "static" stretches, which call for gradually stretching through a muscle's full range of movement until you feel resistance. This gradually loosens muscles without straining them.

6. Avoid high-impact aerobics. Surveys have found that most aerobics instructors and many students suffer injuries to their shins, calves, lower back, ankles, and knees because of the repetitive, jarring movements of jumping to a disco beat. Fortunately, there's a less stressful form of aerobics called low-impact aerobics, which substitutes marching or gliding movements for the jolting up-and-down motion of typical aerobics. At least one foot is almost always on the floor, so the body stays closer to the floor than in conventional aerobics. And arm movement is emphasized to help raise your heart rate sufficiently so the workout is truly aerobic. A well-designed low-impact aerobic routine can easily raise your heart rate enough to provide cardiovascular benefits. Working out more strenuously than that isn't necessary. In fact, it may strain your body excessively.

7. For most people, wearing hand and especially ankle weights isn't advisable while running, jumping, or doing other high-impact activities. The weights can distort your form and balance and can increase the chance of injury to knees, arms, and shoulders unless you have complete control over them. However, light hand weights may be useful in intensifying a low-impact aerobic workout.

8. Don't forget that even the best exercise routine can become risky if you don't begin by warming up and finish by cooling down. All it takes to get started is a few minutes of running in place or brisk walking, followed by some gradual basic stretches. And when you're finishing up, just slow your pace for the last five to ten minutes and gently stretch the major muscle groups you have used.

Source: *University of California Berkeley Wellness Letter,* May 1988, pp. 4–5.

Circuit training is a type of weight training that is often used by those who wish to improve their muscular endurance. Generally speaking, circuit training involves 8 to 15 exercises (called **stations**) using free weights or weight machines. A complete circuit consists of one set of 10 or more repetitions of each exercise. The weight loads used are kept low—55 to 70 percent of the individual's 1 repetition maximum for each exercise. The critical element is that the interval between each exercise is quite brief—approximately 15 seconds. A workout may consist of up to 3 circuits. Although circuit training is particularly useful for increasing muscular endurance, it may be used to increase muscular strength as well, by varying the weights and repetitions.

Circuit training is but one of many forms of weight training. For a more detailed description of some of these training techniques, see the Resource List provided at the end of this volume.

A FLEXIBILITY TRAINING PROGRAM

Flexibility training is a critical but often neglected portion of any training regimen. The goal of flexibility training is to improve the range of motion of a particular joint or group of joints.

Because inadequate flexibility can lead to muscle or joint injury, stretching programs are often prescribed for preventive purposes. (However, despite this common practice, there is no firm agreement as to what constitutes an optimal level of flexibility for preventing injury. [8])

Improvement of flexibility through proper stretching can also improve athletic performance—as well as the ease with which daily activities are accomplished—by increasing the range through which a person can move his or her joints safely and comfortably. It should be noted, though, that extreme flexibility is not always desirable. So-called "hypermobile" joints, for example, may lack stability and hamper performance or predispose a person to injury.

Some professionals believe that stretching may temporarily alleviate some of the muscular soreness experienced both immediately after a workout (*acute muscle soreness*) and hours or days after a workout (*delayed-onset muscle soreness*). There is disagreement on this topic within the fitness field, however, and not all fitness experts believe this is true. There have also been reports of a reduction in stress and muscular tension during and imme-

(continued on p. 107)

Did You Know That . . .

The only difference between male and female muscle is in their relative size, with men's being larger. The sex hormone testosterone plays a key role in muscle growth; though both sexes have this androgen, men have more.

Circuit training: A form of weight training in which participants complete lifting exercises in rapid succession at various stations comprising a "circuit;" particularly suited to increasing muscular endurance, circuit training may also be used to increase muscular strength.

Stations: The term used to identify the exercise activities that together comprise a circuit training program, e.g., a squat or bench press; circuit training exercises may involve either free weights or weight machines.

FIGURE 5.6
A Balanced Strength Program

Calf raises
(calf muscles)

Leg extension
(quadriceps)

Leg curl
(hamstrings)

Bent row
(shoulder, biceps)

Squat
(thighs and hip muscles)

Shown here are 9 strength exercises using barbells and free weights. Each exercise benefits a specific muscle or muscle group. Due to the risk of injury, it is important to seek advice from a trained exercise professional before starting such a program.

Behind-the-neck press
(deltoids)

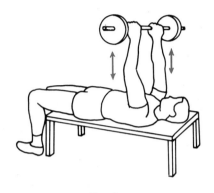

Bench press
(triceps and chest)

Biceps curl
(biceps)

Triceps press
(triceps)

Did You Know That . . .

Walking has recently surpassed swimming as the nation's leading form of exercise.

Tired of running or swimming all the time? More and more people these days alternate the types of sport or exercise they do, and biathlons (two sports) and triathlons (three sports) are catching up to marathons in popularity. This is called cross training—working out regularly at more than one physical activity. Not only is it a way to avoid the boredom of day-in, day-out routine exercise, but it can also provide good overall conditioning, while reducing the risk of injury.

A Better, More Balanced Body

Complementary workouts. Cross training allows you to exercise more muscle groups than a single activity would. For instance, cycling builds your lower body, and swimming works your upper body, so alternating them can help give you the benefits of both while you build aerobic endurance. Similarly, running strengthens the hamstring muscles (located at the rear of the thigh) far more than the quadriceps (at the front of the thigh), a muscle imbalance that may be a factor in some injuries. But by combining cycling, which strengthens the quadriceps, with running, you can work complementary muscle groups in your legs and thus achieve better muscle balance.

Resting your muscles. Overtraining at one sport or activity continually stresses the same muscles and joints, thus increasing the risk of injury. If instead of running every day, you alternate it with swimming every other day, you'll give your leg muscles and joints a needed rest between runs. And if you do hurt your knee while running, you won't have to stop exercising—you can keep on swimming to maintain your aerobic capacity. Or if you pull a shoulder muscle playing tennis, you can give it a rest while you continue to cycle.

Some sports-medicine specialists believe that cross training may also reduce the risk of injury by moderating the "addiction" to a single sport that can result in overtraining. However, competitive cross trainers may fall prey to certain overuse injuries, often as a result of insufficient muscle rest and an unbalanced training schedule.

If you're serious about one particular sport, don't expect cross training to help improve your performance. The plain fact is, you've got to run to become an outstanding runner, swim to win swimming meets. Several studies of the cross trainers who make the headlines—the triathletes who run a marathon, bike a century (100 miles), and swim over two miles all in one day, in heroic events like the Hawaii Ironman triathlon—show that however qualified they may be to take on three events, triathletes don't approach the competitive levels in individual events achieved by single-sport specialists. But in terms of overall fitness, top-class triathletes are some of the best-conditioned athletes in the world.

If you decide to take up cross training, start slowly, as you would any exercise program. The best method is to pair sports that train different parts of your body: swimming with cycling, say, or rowing with running. Instead of three or more 40-minute cycling sessions per week, cycle for 20 minutes and spend the other 20 running, or swim one day and then play tennis the next. If you belong to a health club that has a track, a pool, weight-training machines, and stationary bikes, you'll find cross training a snap.

Source: *University of California Berkeley Wellness Letter,* April 1989, pp. 2–3.

diately after a stretching routine, but these findings have also been the subject of some debate.

General Guidelines for Flexibility Training

Muscles stretch more safely, effectively, and comfortably when the stretching session follows a general warm-up. Thus, at least 5 minutes of brisk walking, light jogging, stationary cycling, or a similarly mild but dynamic activity should precede any stretching session.

The use of a comfortable mat or padded carpet is advisable when performing stretching exercises on the floor. Clothing should allow for ample freedom of movement.

Flexibility is highly specific to individual joints. Therefore, it is necessary to perform a range of exercises in order to cover all of the major joints and muscle groups. Static stretching (discussed in chapter 2) is the preferred mode of stretching. Not only is it simple to perform, but it is also safe and highly effective.

Proper static stretching technique requires easing into the stretched position slowly until some tension is felt in the muscle. The stretch is then held in that position for a minimum of 10 to 30 seconds. During the stretch, breathing should be relaxed and regular. The stretch is ended by easing out of the stretched position slowly and smoothly.

SUMMARY

The guidelines presented in this chapter summarize some of the more common exercises and techniques used to improve fitness in any exercise program. In chapter 6, we outline a stepped approach to a personal fitness program. Using the tips and guidelines in that chapter, you will be able to design your own program—one that reflects your own goals and needs and that helps you to make exercise an integral part of your life. 🔲

6

Making Exercise a Part of Your Life

THE FIRST 5 CHAPTERS of this book have prepared you to make a commitment toward enhanced fitness and well-being. You have become aware of the hazards of a sedentary life-style, the basic principles of fitness, the benefits associated with regular training, and the precautions that should be taken to minimize the risks of injury or other potential problems.

In this chapter we discuss how to develop a fitness program that will meet your personal needs and goals. Like many tasks, devising such a program becomes much more manageable if broken down into a series of steps. That is the approach taken here, and it has several advantages. The first is the one just noted. Dividing a potentially formidable task into several more manageable steps (in this case 5) makes it easier to carry out. Even more important, the steps suggested here are designed to help ensure that the program you devise will be safe and effective. To be sure, there can be no guarantees in such matters. Even the best-designed plan may fail to produce the intended results for one or more reasons that the designer failed to anticipate. Furthermore, there is no such thing as an exercise program that is wholly without risk. On balance, however, the risks associated with any well-designed exercise plan can reasonably be expected to far outweigh those associated with a sedentary life-style.

The remainder of this chapter describes a 5-step approach to exercise that will help you to identify your exercise goals and develop a program for meeting them. After describing these steps, we close by addressing an equally important topic: how to stick with your program.

A STEPPED APPROACH TO A PERSONAL FITNESS PROGRAM

Let's begin with an overview of the steps we will be discussing in the remainder of this chapter. These are as follows:

- Step 1: Obtain medical clearance, if necessary, and determine your initial fitness levels.
- Step 2: Develop goals that are reasonable and attainable.
- Step 3: Choose the appropriate mode(s) of training to realize your goals.
- Step 4: Apply the appropriate frequency, intensity, and duration of training.
- Step 5: Progressively increase frequency, intensity, and duration until your goals are realized.

Step 1: Obtain Medical Clearance, If Necessary, and Determine Your Initial Fitness Levels

While a well-designed exercise program carries few risks for healthy individuals, some people should seek medical advice before beginning to exercise. In general, any person who has a health condition that might limit his or her ability to exercise or that might be made worse by exercise should consult a physician before starting a training program.

For *apparently healthy people*, consulting a physician is optional. The American College of Sports Medicine, for example, advises that such individuals can safely forgo a medical exam or stress test before beginning a moderate exercise program. [1] However, even in the absence of evidence suggesting the need for a complete medical exam, it is advisable to make use of one of the several currently available alternative screening methods before beginning an exercise program. One of the simplest of these is the Physical Activity Readiness Questionnaire (PAR-Q). (See page 110.) The PAR-Q is simple to use and reliable. Anyone who answers "yes" to any of the 6 questions in the PAR-Q should consult a doctor before proceeding with any exercise program. [2]

The ACSM advises a medical exam or graded exercise test for persons of any age who fall into one of several "higher risk" categories. These include anyone who has 2 or more of the risk factors for coronary artery disease (see chapter 1), and anyone who has symptoms of cardiovascular or pulmonary (lung) disease.

It's also wise to consult a physician to avoid forms of exercise that might worsen other existing medical conditions. For exam-

Did You Know That . . .

Low-impact aerobics can be a great starting point for the beginning exerciser or one who is not well-conditioned or flexible.

Table 6.1 Physical Activity Readiness Questionnaire (PAR-Q)

1. Has your doctor ever said you have heart trouble?	yes [ ]	no [ ]
2. Do you frequently suffer from pain in your chest?	yes [ ]	no [ ]
3. Do you often feel faint or have spells of severe dizziness?	yes [ ]	no [ ]
4. Has a doctor ever told you that you have a bone or joint problem such as arthritis that has been aggravated by exercise, or might be made worse with exercise?	yes [ ]	no [ ]
5. Is there a good physical reason not mentioned here why you should not follow an activity program even if you wanted to?	yes [ ]	no [ ]
6. Are you over age 65 and not accustomed to vigorous exercise?	yes [ ]	no [ ]

Source: Modified from *PAR-Q Validation Report,* British Columbia Department of Health, 1975.

Exercise poses no special hazard for most people. Some people, however, should obtain medical advice before starting to exercise. To determine if you are one of these people, take a few minutes to answer the 6 questions listed above. If you answer "yes" to any of them, you should consult a physician before proceeding further.

ple, weak joints may make running, tennis, basketball, or even golf off-limits. Asthmatics should use caution when exercising in cold, dry environments or when irritants (pollution or pollen) are present in the air. People with back problems may have difficulty with cardiovascular or strength-oriented activities that put strain on the lower back muscles. And even low-intensity exertion by someone who has poor flexibility can lead to muscle or joint injury.

In general, it is best to err on the side of caution. If there is any question about the necessity for a medical evaluation, by all means see your physician. The important point here is not that preexisting conditions should prevent people from exercising. On the contrary, while any health problem should be taken into account when designing an exercise program, there is no reason that individuals who aren't in perfect health cannot exercise. To

(continued on p. 112)

What Is an Exercise Stress Test?

A common concern among people soon to undergo an exercise stress test—especially those who are inactive or not in good shape, or who already have symptoms of heart disease—is that they will be pushed into a workout so strenuous that it will itself bring about a heart attack or, at the least, chest pain. In fact, the goal of an exercise stress test is to determine just what your heart is capable of—not what is too much for it.

Many people over 50 undergo a stress test each year (see box at right). According to Medicare statistics, over 600,000 Americans had a stress test in 1989—up 22% from just three years ago. Like most tests, the procedure is not risk-free—but it is *low* risk. The risk of a heart attack during a stress test is less than 1 in 500; the risk of dying is less than 1 in 10,000. The test is not going to require you to run a mile if you get winded going up two flights of stairs. Rather, it is designed to determine just what level of activity is within bounds for your heart—be it walking a block or running a marathon. During the test, you will be continually monitored for any possible cardiac trouble. And you will be able to stop the test if you have any significant chest pain. (However, it is normal to feel fatigued, somewhat breathless, and sweaty during the test, as you would during any exercise.)

What it measures

Coronary artery disease (CAD) is due to the buildup of fatty plaque in the heart's arteries, and is the leading cause of heart attacks. As the arteries become progressively narrowed by plaque, less blood can be pumped through them, so less oxygen reaches the heart. In the early stages of CAD, the reduced blood supply may still be comfortably sufficient for nonstrenuous activity. But CAD may make itself known when you exercise, as this increases the demand for oxygen beyond what the diseased arteries can supply. If the oxygen deficiency is severe enough, it can cause the heart-muscle pain known as angina. Lesser deficiencies of oxygen may cause

Who needs an exercise stress test?

Usually, there is no need to have a stress test if you don't have any cardiac symptoms and have no particular risk for heart disease. In healthy people, the test produces too many false positives (indications that something is amiss when everything is alright), which lead to unnecessary worry and expense. . . . However, stress testing is a valuable screen if you fall into one of the following categories:

- You have a family history of heart disease (relatives have died from heart disease before the age of 55).
- You have diabetes, hypertension, are obese (30% or more overweight), or smoke.
- You have symptoms of coronary artery disease, such as chest pain during exertion.
- You have been sedentary and plan to start a vigorous exercise program.
- You have had heart surgery or a heart attack (the test will help determine prognosis and an appropriate heart-strengthening program for you).

changes in blood pressure, heart rate, and heart rhythm, and may produce certain changes on an electrocardiogram. (An ECG, or EKG, as it is called, depicts the electrical activity produced by the heart. Leads attached to your body during a stress test conduct these electrical charges to a machine that prints out a tracing of them.) An abnormal ECG during an exercise stress test generally indicates that further tests are in order to pinpoint just which arteries are blocked and by how much.

Walking through the test

A stress test may be performed in your doctor's office, at the hospital, or at a freestanding test center. Wherever, it requires a special facility equipped to handle any emergency that might arise, and should be performed by trained technicians. To meet guidelines set by the American Heart Association, all personnel performing stress tests should be trained in cardiopulmonary resuscitation (CPR), and at least one of the two technicians in the room must be trained in advanced life-support. A physician must be on the premises at all times.

Before the test, a resting ECG will be done to check for any abnormalities in the heart even without added stress, and to provide a basis for comparison during the exercise. Resting blood pressure and pulse are also measured, and are continually monitored during the procedure. ECG leads are also kept in place throughout the exercise and for 10 minutes or so afterwards, since some changes may take that long to appear.

Exertion may be produced in different ways: a stair-climbing machine, a stationary bicycle, a treadmill, or a machine for arm exercises. The treadmill is used most often, but patients with arthritis or other problems that make walking difficult will be offered a bicycle, which places less strain on the joints.

The test proceeds slowly and gradually. Usually, you exercise at each level for three minutes. Then the amount of exertion is increased by raising either the speed of the machine or the grade of incline. For example, on a treadmill stress test, you start out walking slowly, progress to fast walking, then to jogging, then to jogging uphill.

Two different procedures may be used. In the more common, the maximum symptom-limited test, you proceed with progressively more strenuous exercise until *moderate* chest pain, fatigue, or severe shortness of breath occurs; then the test is stopped.

The other method is called the submaximum heart-rate limited protocol. In this version, the amount of exercise you are expected to do is predetermined, based on your age and health; the test is concluded when you reach this predetermined level (unless symptoms occur or there is a clear change in ECG, in which case the test will be terminated earlier).

Interpreting the results

If you don't have heart disease, you should be able to exercise up to your target heart rate, or THR (which is determined by your pulse), without undue symptoms or changes in blood pressure or ECG. You can estimate your THR using this simple formula: (220 minus your age) × 0.9 (for example, if you are 50, your THR is (220 − 50) × 0.9, or 153). The more fit will need a more strenuous workout to reach their THR. Others will achieve their THR at very moderate levels of exercise. In any case, exercising at your THR requires effort. You may feel dizzy, light-headed, and fatigued. These are all normal symptoms that even Olympians experience when they reach their maximum heart rate. However, as long as you reach your THR with no chest pain or unusual blood pressure or ECG changes, your heart is probably in good shape.

Inability to reach your THR may indicate that your heart is not operating at its fullest capacity. Further tests, such as a thallium scan (in which a radioactive dye is injected into your arm and its passage is traced through your heart during an exercise stress test to find out just which areas are involved), are likely to be ordered to pinpoint the cause of the problem and so determine treatment.

Source: *Johns Hopkins Medical Letter* December, 1991, pp. 6–7.

do so safely, however, they should first seek appropriate medical advice and then observe the recommended guidelines.

Bear in mind that some discomfort—such as muscle soreness or joint stiffness—is common, particularly at the beginning of an exercise program. However, chest, joint, muscle, or other moderate to severe pain that persists is a signal that should not be ignored, no matter when it occurs or to whom. A sharp pain that develops in the ankle region during an aerobics class, for example, may indicate an injury to the Achilles tendon. If this occurs, the activity should be stopped and the injury treated using the R.I.C.E. method (discussed in chapter 4) or another appropriate form of treatment.

High-risk participants—those with chronic diseases—need to develop an ability to distinguish between transitory symptoms of discomfort and those that may indicate more serious problems. Again, when in doubt, seek medical advice.

Once confident that you can safely pursue an exercise program, it is time to determine your level of physical fitness. The fitness assessment has several purposes: (1) to gather baseline data in order to establish realistic goals; (2) to assist in choosing the proper mode(s), frequency, intensity, and duration of activity; and (3) to determine any possible health risk not uncovered by the medical exam (e.g., flexibility problems, muscular weaknesses, or skeletal problems).

A fitness assessment can be obtained from a variety of sources including colleges, community centers, and fitness clubs. Preferably, any such test should be administered by a qualified individual. If this is not possible, you will have to rely on one or more of the numerous articles or books on this topic, some of which are listed in the Resource Appendix to this volume. (See also "How Fit Are You?" on pages 114 and 115.)

Step 2: Develop Goals That Are Reasonable and Attainable

Fitness goals must be realistic. They must be reasonable and reachable, and must take into account an individual's initial level of fitness and other limitations, such as age, time constraints, financial resources, and climate. Your set of goals should address, at a minimum, any areas where there is clear need for improvement (for example, "improve aerobic fitness"), as well as any other objectives that are important to you personally (such as "lose weight but not muscle"). A balanced set of goals will be based on the basic fitness principles outlined in chapter 2.

Unreasonable expectations will doom any exercise program before it starts. A program designed around overly ambitious goals is likely to lead to injury, discouragement, or both, and can ultimately result in a loss of fitness. For example, a 50-year-old arthritic man who is just beginning an exercise program should not list "competing in the Ironman Triathlon" as a short-term goal. For him, such a goal is virtually unreachable.

(continued on p. 115)

Did You Know That . . .

Exercise tapes are much in demand on the videocassette market right now, carrying advice for would-be exercisers of various sizes, shapes, and tastes.

How Fit Are You?

Every day millions of flabby Americans suddenly throw on sweatsuits and plunge into sports. . . . Fitness experts recommend that you find out what shape you're in before trying to get into shape.

Remember, the following charts are only guidelines. The key should always be individual fitness. Each person must consider heredity and medical history. Always be sure to check with your physician before beginning any fitness program.

Flexibility

Flexibility refers to the elasticity and smooth easy movement of the joints and muscles. The book *Sports Fitness and Training* states "Back, hip, and hamstring flexibility are most important in sports." If your body is flexible, you'll feel more at ease and avoid injuries, especially debilitating back problems. To test for flexibility of the hamstrings (muscles in the back of your legs), hip and lower back muscles, the Official YMCA Fitness Program suggests the sit-and-reach test. Sit on the floor with your feet in front of you, about 12 inches apart. Tape a yardstick to the floor between your legs lengthwise; the 15-inch mark should be about at your heel (that means the 1-inch mark should be at your knees). Keeping legs straight, lean forward slowly and reach as far ahead as you can on the yardstick. Record where your fingertips reach and check results.

Excellent	24–27 inches
Good	21–23 inches
Average	17–20 inches
Fair	13–16 inches
Poor	0–12 inches

Strength

[Ed. note: Although more properly a test of muscular endurance as defined in this book, the strength test described here is useful because, unlike the standard test for muscular strength—known as the one repetition maximum (1RM) test—it can be safely performed at home with the assistance of a trained spotter.]

Strength refers to the amount of force that can be exerted by a single muscle contraction. Practically speaking, it can mean being able to lift a hefty 25-pound toddler. As you grow stronger,

you will find many tasks easier; your posture will improve, and you'll be less susceptible to injury.

Although some parts of your body may be stronger than others (women tend to have weaker upper bodies than men), a sit-up test is a good way to measure strength. With knees bent, hands behind head, do as many sit-ups as you can within a one-minute period.

Excellent	46–54
Good	35–45
Average	21–34
Fair	10–20
Poor	2–9

Cardiovascular fitness

Cardiovascular endurance measures the capability of the heart and lungs to deliver oxygen to exercising muscles. A person in good cardiovascular condition can do many exercises, like swimming, running, biking, or climbing stairs, for extended periods without becoming tired.

The National Institute of Fitness and Sport recommends this simple at-home step test to measure recovery rate. All you need is a bench or steep step.

To begin, step up on the bench first with your left foot and then your right foot. Continue to go up and down for three minutes. At the end of three minutes, wait a minute and then take your pulse for 30 seconds. Wait another minute and then take your pulse again for 30 seconds. Take your pulse again after waiting another minute (three minutes will have passed since exercise ended). Add your three times together to get your recovery rate. See [below] for recovery rate chart.

Cardiovascular Fitness

Excellent	126
	130
	135
Good	141
	147
	153

Average	158
	164
	170
Fair	176
	181
	187
Poor	193
	199
	204

Body Fat

Everyone needs some body fat. Fat in healthy humans ranges from 5 to 40 percent, according to *Sports Fitness and Training*. Anyone with more than 40 percent fat is considered obese. Women by nature have more fat than men. Besides your waist, fat tends to accumulate on the hips, sides, arms, thighs and chest.

To measure your body fat, The National Institute of Fitness and Sport says stand and pinch the fold of skin around your waist and measure the depth of the fold.

Very low fat	less than $1/4$ in.
Low fat	$1/4$ to $1/2$ in.
Average	$1/2$ to $3/4$
Above normal	$3/4$ to 1 in.
Very high	over one inch

Beware beginner mistakes

California fitness trainer Bill Calkins offers these five common mistakes frequently made by beginners.

1. Unrealistic expectations: Not everyone can look like Cybil Shepherd or Tom Selleck. You have to work within your own genetic limitations, looking the best that you can.
2. Improper instruction: You can't achieve your goals unless you use proper technique. Have a program designed for you by a qualified instructor.
3. Impatience: It takes 6–12 months to get into decent shape. Many people are upset if it doesn't happen in 6–12 days. Be patient. It takes time.
4. Too much too soon: In a yearning for quick results, many beginners overdo it in the first few weeks. This can lead to injury and a quick end to your program.
5. Low priority: Exercise must become part of your lifestyle. Putting it off until you get around to it assures that you won't. Plan a specific time of day to exercise.

Source: *St. Raphael's Better Health Letter,* September/October 1987, pp. 10–12.

It is often more difficult for younger, healthier persons to be aware of their physical limitations and thus to avoid setting goals that are not excessive. For instance, a 23-year-old novice exerciser who is 30 pounds over her ideal weight might want to lose 30 pounds by the time she goes on vacation in August (4 weeks away). She might also wish to test her progress by running a 10-K (10-kilometer, or 6.2-mile) road race in September (8 weeks away).

These goals are inappropriate for several reasons. Our exerciser is trying for too much, too soon. Losing 30 pounds of body weight in 4 weeks is likely to be physiologically impossible. Attempts to do so will result in dietary restrictions that far exceed those viewed as prudent by most experts. To lose even 8 pounds a month requires considerable thought, discipline, and effort. This woman would be better advised to make sure that any

Did You Know That . . .

I t's wise to schedule your exercise session at a time of
day when your natural rhythms
are most likely to be compatible
with exercising.

diet plan she adopts is nutritionally sound, that it is accompanied by an appropriate exercise program, and that it includes a commitment to the kind of life-style and behavioral changes that will ensure the weight stays off once it has been lost. Moreover, she should plan to take between 3 and 6 months to lose her 30 pounds.

In addition, since this woman is currently overweight and is embarking on a first attempt at exercise, her expectation of reaching a level of fitness, in 2 months, that would permit her even to complete the 10-K race distance is simply foolhardy. A serious attempt to meet this objective is all but certain to result in discouragement or injury or both. Again, the goal is too much, too soon. A more sensible approach would be to train more slowly, gradually increasing distance and intensity over at least 6 months. After that period of time, she might enter a shorter-distance race just to participate, but only provided she can run that distance easily in training. And under no circumstances should she try to be seriously competitive in her first race. Eventually, she will find her level of competitive performance improving as her fitness and experience grow. This is a slow process, but it is sure.

These principles should be kept in mind when you devise your own fitness goals. The objective is a set of goals that are both realistic and attainable within a reasonable period of time. Because of their importance to your exercise program, these goals should be written down, constantly reviewed, and periodically revised, following a procedure such as the one listed below:

A. Start by writing down a list of your long-term goals. Examples of two such goals (taken from the discussion at the beginning of this section) are to "improve aerobic fitness" and "lose weight but not muscle."

B. Review these goals while keeping in mind the results of any fitness and medical health evaluations. Do your goals make sense in light of those evaluations? Do they take into account any existing medical conditions? Do they address all the fitness components, including those where you are weakest? Do they allow for balanced progress?

C. Finalize your list of fitness goals based on your responses to the questions listed above. If possible, this list should be reviewed–and refined, if necessary–by an exercise professional, or at least by someone who has had experience with training programs, to ensure that the goals listed are well-balanced, reasonable, and reachable.

D. Then, to help meet your long-term goals, develop a series of

(continued on p. 118)

Typical Fitness Goals and Strategies for Attaining Them

GOAL:
Run a 10-kilometer (6.2-mile) race in 6 months (improve cardiovascular endurance).

RECOMMENDATION:
This requires a cardiovascular exercise program incorporating jogging and then running. If it is a first race, training to complete the distance is more important than to improve speed. The program should emphasize distance running but should include other aerobic and muscular endurance exercises.

GOAL:
Lose weight but maintain as much muscle as possible.

RECOMMENDATION:
This requires a cardiovascular exercise program and a diet that will promote weight loss. Dieting will reduce muscle mass. But if dietary restrictions are combined with a supplementary cardiovascular exercise program, the loss of fat-free mass will be minimized.

GOAL:
Maintain current weight but decrease percentage of body fat.

RECOMMENDATION:
This requires a combination of cardiovascular training and weight training. A low-fat, complex carbohydrate diet is also recommended.

GOAL:
Increase strength and muscle size.

RECOMMENDATION:
This requires a weight-training program with an emphasis on higher intensity (> −75 percent of 1 repetition maximum or 4–6RM), a moderate number of repetitions (6–8), and 3 or more sets of each exercise. Supplementary cardiovascular exercise is also advisable.

GOAL:
Improve muscular endurance.

RECOMMENDATION:
This requires a combination of weight training, body resistance, and muscular endurance exercises. The emphasis should be on lower intensity (50–75 percent of 1RM) and higher repetitions (12 to 20 per set). Regular cardiovascular exercise will also help the affected muscle groups.

GOAL:	Become more flexible.
RECOMMENDATION:	This requires a balanced flexibility program. Exercises should address all of the major muscle groups and joints in the body. The stretching program should follow a warm-up and should be composed of static stretches held for a minimum of 10 seconds.

short- and intermediate-term exercise goals that can be used to help determine the appropriate mode(s), frequency, intensity, and duration of exercise (as described in the discussion of Steps 3 and 4 below).

Examples of reasonable fitness goals and some appropriate recommendations for achieving them are shown in "Typical Fitness Goals and Strategies for Attaining Them" on pages 117 and 118.

Step 3: Choose the Appropriate Mode(s) of Training to Realize Your Goals

Which form of exercise to pursue is largely a matter of personal taste. Some people like more active and intense forms of exercise, such as basketball or running. Some like to exercise with other people, as in an aerobics class or on a volleyball team. Others prefer to exercise alone, perhaps using weight-training equipment or following a videotaped exercise program.

There are so many different modes of exercise that virtually everyone can find a number of activities that are well-suited to his or her interests and long-term goals. Furthermore, a little variety can help make an exercise program more enjoyable, and is particularly useful for anyone who wishes to work on several components of fitness at the same time—muscular strength and aerobic fitness, for example. Occasionally, factors other than personal preference will determine the form or level of exercise you should pursue. Medical concerns are probably the most common of these, but other possible considerations include location, expense, climate, and time of year.

The most important consideration in selecting your mode(s) of exercise, however, is your exercise goals. If your primary goal is to improve your cardiovascular fitness, for example, activities such as walking, jogging, swimming, or aerobic dance are reasonable choices. To enhance your muscular strength, your primary

(continued on p. 120)

FIGURE 6.1
Vary Your Routine

Source: American Heart Association.

The variety of available exercise programs and facilities makes it possible to choose activities suited to your goals and to explore new choices when your interests change.

Did You Know That . . .

Some advisors say beginning runners should run for 20 to 30 minutes at least 3 days but not more than 5 days a week.

options are various kinds of resistance training using either free weights or machines. Stretching exercises are a common feature of flexibility training programs, and resistance training and calesthenics are often useful to help improve muscular endurance. These and a variety of other options are listed in Table 6.2 on page 121. (See also "16 Ways to Work Out: The Pros and Cons" on pages 122 and 123.)

While the modes of exercise listed in Table 6.2 by no means exhaust the full range of possibilities, they are a useful starting point. Whatever your chosen forms of exercise, it is critical that they be keyed to your long-term goals and that the resulting program be a balanced one that addresses the important components of fitness.

Step 4: Apply the Appropriate Frequency, Intensity, and Duration of Training

Once you are sure of your goals and have settled upon an appropriate mode of exercise, you will need to determine an appropriate frequency, intensity, and duration for your proposed exercise program. The ACSM guidelines mentioned in the previous chapter are a useful guide for beginners. A set of basic rules of thumb for the beginning exerciser derived from these guidelines is as follows:

- *Frequency*: An initial frequency of 3 exercise sessions per week, increasing as fitness improves to as much as 5 sessions per week.
- *Intensity*: An initial intensity of from 50 to 75 percent of maximum heart rate reserve or a perceived exertion rating of "somewhat hard" or "hard" (from 13 to 16 on the 20-point RPE scale; see page 91).
- *Duration*: An initial duration of 15 to 20 minutes of activity per exercise session at the target heart rate, to be increased gradually as fitness increases.

Like all rules of thumb, these are general principles. What they mean in practice—particularly in the case of intensity—will depend on a variety of factors, including one's initial level of fitness. A level of activity that seems quite intense to an overweight, sedentary person may seem insignificant to someone who is already in excellent condition.

Keep in mind, too, that intensity, frequency, and duration need to be continually monitored and adjusted if you wish to

(continued on p. 123)

Table 6.2 Selected Modes of Exercise by Fitness Component

Fitness Component	Appropriate Modes of Exercise

Cardiovascular Fitness	Walking
	Jogging/Running
	Cycling
	Swimming
	Aerobic Dance
	Bench Aerobics
	Nordic (Cross-Country) Skiing
	Cardiovascular Exercise Machines:
	    Stair Climbers
	    Stationary Cycles (Ergometers)
	    Rowing Machines

Muscular Endurance	Calisthenics/Floor Exercises:
	    Examples include abdominal curls and push-ups
	Exercises using light hand-held weights, bands, ankle weights
	Circuit Weight Training:
	    Using exercises listed in muscular strength section, but with lighter weights and high repetitions

Muscular Strength	Resistance Training With Free Weights:
	    Examples include squat, lunge, bench press, military press, bent row, biceps curl, triceps press, back extensions
	Resistance Training With Machines:
	    Examples include leg press, leg extension, leg curl, calf machine, bench press, lat pull, shoulder press, biceps curl, triceps press, back extensions

Flexibility	Static Stretching Exercises: Examples include neck stretch, shoulder stretch, straddle, standing quadriceps stretch, supine hamstring stretch, calf stretch

Different fitness goals require different modes of exercise. Shown here is a sampling of the modes of exercise that are appropriate to various components of fitness.

16 Ways to Work Out: The Pros and Cons

Choosing a Workout

Can any one exercise give you the ultimate fitness benefits? Not according to new exercise guidelines from the American College of Sports Medicine (ACSM). The latest guidelines—the first update since 1978—recommend a regimen that pushes up more than just your heart rate; they now put more emphasis on building muscle strength and endurance. How to get overall conditioning? Mix and match your activities.

The table below can help. It shows the benefits and costs of 16 popular activities. Decide which sports suit your taste, pace and pocketbook, then weigh the dollar costs and injury rates against the fitness benefits.

Our panel of six experts rated each activity on a ten-point scale. *Aerobics,* which contributes to life-preserving cardiovascular health, gets top rating, up to four stars. *Fat loss,* or how efficiently the activity burns fat, gets a maximum of one

ACTIVITY	BENEFITS						COSTS		
Maximum Score	Aerobics ★★★★	Fat Loss ★	Strength ★★	Muscle Endurance ★★	Flexi-bility ★	Total 10	Injury Rate	Workout Time (min.)	Start-Up Costs
Swimming	★★★★	★	★	★★	★	9	Low	30	$20–$975*
Cross-Country Skiing (outdoors)	★★★★	★	★	★★	½	8½	Medium	25	$100–$200
Circuit Weight Training	★★½	½	★★	★★	½	7½	Medium	30	$200–$675*
Running	★★★★	★	½	★½		7	High	25	$40–$85
Aerobic Dance	★★★	★	★	★½	½	7	High	35	$30–$675*
Cycling (outdoors)	★★★½	★	★	★		6½	High**	35	$150–$750
Rowing machine	★★★	★	★	★½		6½	Medium	35	$100–$400
Walking	★★★½	★	½	★		6	Low	45	$40–$85
Stair Climbing (machine)	★★★½	★	½	★		6	Low	25	$120–$2,000
Golf (carrying clubs)	★★½	★	½	★½	½	6	Low	45	$200–$725
Rope Skipping	★★★½	½	½	★		5½	Medium	25	$45–$80
Racquetball/ Squash	★★★	★	½	½	½	5½	Medium	35	$70–$815*
Basketball/ Soccer	★★★	½	½	★		5	High	40	$30–$125
Weight Training	★		★★	★½	½	5	Medium	60	$130–$675*
Tennis (singles)	★★½	½	½	½	½	4½	Medium	45	$80–$315
Calisthenics	★½		★	★	★	4½	Low	60	$40–$55

*Upper range includes club fees.

**Includes collisions without helmet.

star. *Strength* gets up to two stars; so does *muscle endurance,* which helps you repeat an activity. *Flexibility*—whether the activity helps you stay limber—gets a maximum of one star.

These ratings represent a shift in values from what the same experts told *Changing Times* three years ago, when aerobics was the last word in fitness. Aerobics gets fewer maximum points, and strength and muscle endurance get more. That shift reflects the ACSM's latest findings, which link strength training with better posture and prevention of osteoporosis. "Muscle just fades away if it's not being used," says Michael Pollock, a panelist and key author of the ACSM's report.

Panelist Paul Ribisl, who at 51 is a longtime runner, figures that his body would be better off today if he'd had more strength and muscle training: "When I was 20 or 30, I never had to worry about muscular endurance, never lost it. But it hits home as you get older. It means a better quality of life."

You can meet the ACSM's guidelines for a well-rounded fitness program by interspersing, say, weight lifting with running or calisthenics with swimming (which was also the highest-ranking activity the last time we rated the activities).

As you consult the chart, remember that the benefits you get hinge on two things: the time you take and the level of intensity you put forth. For example, for cardiovascular fitness, work out at your target heart rate at least three times a week. Or simply try to burn 300 calories in each workout. (That goal is reflected in the *workout time* on the chart.) Most people can keep injuries down and fitness benefits up by exercising for longer periods of time at lower intensity levels. Always remember to warm up and cool down. That will put you in great shape.

The Panelists
Edward Howley, Ph.D., professor in Department of Human Performance in Sports Studies at the University of Tennessee at Knoxville. **David Johnson, M.D.,** past medical consultant to the President's Council on Physical Fitness and Sports. **Robert Nirschl, M.D.,** orthopedic consultant to the President's Council on Physical Fitness and Sports. **Michael Pollock, Ph.D.,** director of the Center for Exercise Science at the University of Florida at Gainesville. **Paul Ribisl, Ph.D.,** former chairman of the preventive and rehabilitative committee of the American College of Sports Medicine. **Thomas Whitehead, Ed.D.,** senior director of corporate services for the National Institute for Fitness and Sport.

Source: *Changing Times,* August 1990, pp. 94–96.

reach your long-term fitness goals. If you don't make adjustments, you will quickly find that your level of progress will stagnate, and your fitness improvement program will become a fitness maintenance program. To be sure, improvement will cease at some point in any case, for everyone's ability to improve his or her level of fitness has some finite limit (which can and does vary from individual to individual). The crucial point, however, is to make sure that improvement continues until you have realized your original goals.

Of the 3 variables discussed here, intensity is perhaps the most crucial one. Research suggests, in fact, that the magnitude of the training effect is more closely related to intensity than to any other factor. [3] It is important, therefore, to ensure that your

Did You Know That . . .

Advanced runners should be running 5 or 6 days a week, with weekly mileage ranging from 25 to 60 miles, depending on whether or not they are training for a marathon.

initial level of intensity is neither too low to produce results nor too high to be risky. Because of this, and because the appropriate level of intensity will almost certainly increase steadily, particularly during the early phase of a training program, it should be carefully monitored at all times.

Proper duration is also important. While no threshold duration for optimal cardiovascular improvement has been identified, longer duration is generally associated with measurable improvements in fitness. Furthermore, increasing the duration of one's training can probably offset a decrease in intensity. [4] The downside to all this is that it may take a very large increase in duration to offset a very low level of intensity. In addition, increasing the duration of exercise activities also increases the exposure to injury risk. Still, for those who wish to improve their fitness but cannot work out at a high level of intensity, the answer may be to extend the duration of the exercise session—to work longer rather than harder.

Much the same is true of frequency. That is to say, all other things being equal, increasing frequency can offset a relatively low level of intensity. A high frequency—5 to 7 days a week—is particularly recommended for those who are exercising as part of a weight control program. [5] The primary reason for this is that increasing frequency also increases caloric expenditure, which is particularly important to the success of a weight control program. For most other purposes, however, increases in frequency do not seem to produce significant results. Given this, the customary practice—common to most training programs—of exercising 3 days a week, with a rest day between 2 workout days, is a reasonable model.

Once you have determined the appropriate frequency, duration, and intensity for each of the activities in your program, you are ready to pull together an exercise plan that is tailored to your needs and abilities. It is a good idea to do this in writing, using a form such as the Personal Plan for Weight Training shown in Figure 6.2 on page 125.

Step 5: Progressively Increase Frequency, Intensity, and Duration Until Your Goals Are Realized

Establishing a personal exercise plan is, of course, just the beginning. While a good start is essential to any successful exercise program, just starting is not enough. You need to continue, and more than that, if you wish to achieve your long-term goals, you need to continually monitor your progress and make adjustments in your plan as needed.

(continued on p. 126)

FIGURE 6.2
Personal Plan for Weight Train

Days per week _____

Region of Body Exercised	Exercise(s)	Intensity	Se
Compound lower extremity			
1.			
2.			
Fronts of thighs (quadriceps)			
1.			
2.			
Backs of thighs (hamstrings)			
1.			
2.			
Calves			
1.			
2.			
Chest			
1.			
2.			
Shoulders			
1.			
2.			
Upper back			
1.			
2.			
Arms (biceps/triceps)			
1.			
2.			
Abdominal muscles			
1.			
2.			
Low back			
1.			
2.			

Shown here is a sample worksheet for a weight-training program. A form like this is a useful tool when designing any exercise program.

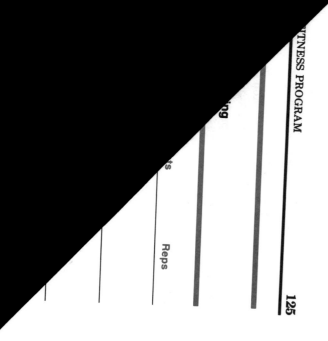

e some allowance for progress from
our initial plan should provide for
es in intensity, frequency, and dura-
s. Here too, a form such as the one
helpful.

any program it describes, should be
ess goals. Figures 6.4 and 6.5 depict
, one for cardiovascular fitness and
le both use similar forms, there are
se 2 programs. The running program
designed for someone who wants to
cular fitness, and it features a steady
tance (listed in the last column) over
g, as it does, a high-impact activity
o its purpose but not appropriate for

gram described in Figure 6.5 is de-
primary goal is weight control. This

FIGURE 6.3

Cardiovascular Program Worksheet

Week	Mode	Intensity (Target Heart Rate)	Frequency (Days/Week)	Duration (Minutes)	Distance (Miles/Week)	Energy (Calories)
1						
2						
3						
4						
5						
6						
7						
8						

A form like the one shown here is useful for designing an exercise program in which frequency, duration, and intensity change over time.

FIGURE 6.4
Sample Exercise Program for Cardiovascular Fitness

Week	Mode	Intensity (% Max Heart Rate Reserve)	Frequency (Days/Week)	Duration (Minutes)	Distance (Miles/Week)
1	Running	65–75%	4	20	9
2	Running	65–75%	4	25	11
3	Running	70–80%	4	30	14
4	Running	70–80%	5	30	17
5	Running	75–85%	5	35	20.5
6	Running	75–85%	5	40	24
7	Running	75–85%	5	45	26
8	Running	75–85%	5	50	30

Shown here is a running-based program designed to improve cardiovascular fitness. It features gradual increases in intensity, frequency, duration, and weekly mileage.

program features a less strenuous form of activity than that in Figure 6.4–walking rather than running. The differences between the 2 programs can be summarized as follows:

- *Frequency*: Although the frequency of the 2 programs is initially the same, the frequency of the weight-control program rapidly increases to 7 days per week, whereas the cardiovascular program peaks out at 5 days per week.
- *Duration*: The duration of the weight-control program is greater than that of the cardiovascular program throughout the 8-week period depicted in Figures 6.4 and 6.5.
- *Intensity*: While their initial levels of intensity are equal, the intensity level of the cardiovascular fitness program gradually increases whereas that of the weight-control program does not.

As these 2 sample programs suggest, there can and will be considerable differences among exercise programs. This is because any effective exercise program must be personalized. That is, it must be suited both to the individual and to his or her purposes, as we have noted. An understanding of this basic principle is essential to the design of any exercise program. So, too, is the notion of progression–continuous monitoring and adjustments to meet your long term-goals.

FIGURE 6.5
Sample Exercise Program for Weight Control

Week	Mode	Intensity (% Max Heart Rate Reserve)	Frequency (Days/Week)	Duration (Minutes)	Energy Cost (Calories/Week)
1	Walking	65–75%	4	40	960
2	Walking	65–75%	4	50	1200
3	Walking	65–75%	5	50	1500
4	Walking	65–75%	5	60	1800
5	Walking	65–75%	6	60	2160
6	Walking	65–75%	7	60	2520
7	Walking	65–75%	7	60	2520
8	Maintenance!				

This sample exercise program for weight control features a constant level of intensity, accompanied by gradual increases in frequency and duration. It is primarily designed to increase caloric expenditure while minimizing injury risk.

INTEGRATING EXERCISE INTO YOUR DAILY LIFE

A healthy life and exercise go together. The knowledge and awareness that come with participating in a well-designed exercise program can often help provide the motivation needed to make life-style changes that promote better health.

But consistent participation in an exercise program can be difficult. Modern life is busy. The demands of school, work, family and friends, and community can overwhelm even the most determined and capable individuals at times, making it difficult to keep up with seemingly less pressing matters such as exercise. Evidence of this can be found in the fact that only about 20 percent of Americans are exercising at levels recommended by the U.S. Department of Health and Human Services. [6]

Despite these discouraging statistics, it *is* possible to construct a healthier way of living. A successful exercise program depends on the establishment of reasonable training goals, the sensible application of the basic principles of fitness, an awareness of the risks and benefits of the various forms of exercise, and, perhaps above all, a common-sense approach to day-to-day training.

(continued on p. 131)

29 Tips for Staying With It

You may help someone begin an exercise program today, or start one yourself. Unfortunately, over half the people who start today won't be exercising six months from now.

I feel the No. 1 exercise challenge is staying with it. Reason: Epidemiological studies have shown that the key to improving your health is to adopt a lifelong program. With exercise, it's consistency that counts.

Medical experts know why people *should* exercise, and so does most of the public. In fact, the public's growing belief in exercise makes it hard to determine how many people actually work out and how often.

American Health has worked with Gallup pollsters in a series of national surveys on the meaning of health and fitness. They've found we're divided into three groups: Those in the lower third exercise less than an hour and a half a week and seem content at that level. The top third, mostly athletes and health club members, exercise five hours or more a week, and feel good about it.

To me, the interesting people are in the middle group. Most are convinced of the benefits of exercise but don't work out consistently. They start and stop, then feel guilty. They blame their work load, they get injured, they get bored.

The medical research on staying with it is classified under these ominous terms: adherence and compliance. One sounds like a moral problem, the other like a cop's command. But in spite of this handicap, there's now a first-rate book on research in this field: *Exercise Adherence* (Human Kinetics Publishers), by Rod Dishman, a University of Georgia sport psychologist.

From Dishman's work, a variety of published scientific articles, and research in our own exercise physiology lab at the University of Massachusetts medical school, I've come up with 29 tips to help exercisers stick with it:

1. Know the stakes. Lack of exercise makes you almost twice as likely to develop coronary heart disease, according to the Centers for Disease Control. Avoiding all exercise increases your risk about as much as smoking one pack of cigarettes a day.

2. Chart out a specific, realistic plan. Sit down with someone the day you decide to begin exercising, preferably a doctor or fitness instructor, and map out an exercise agenda. It's easier with planners like *The Health Benefits of Exercise,* a pamphlet reprint from *The Physician and Sports Medicine.* (For a copy, write: Life Fitness Special Reports, 9601 Geronimo Rd., Irvine, CA 92718.)

3. Get a cholesterol test the day before starting, then again about 10 weeks later. You'll be hearing more about cholesterol now that the American Heart Association has launched its National Cholesterol Education Project. To use cholesterol readings as a motivator, it's important to measure both total cholesterol and the ratio of high-density lipoproteins (HDL), the "good" cholesterol, to low-density lipoproteins (LDL), the "bad" cholesterol. Exercise may not affect total cholesterol without dietary changes, but it's been shown to boost your HDL readings. Improvement in your readings can begin to register within a month and should definitely be present within two months if you stay with exercise.

4. Find a bench mark for an exercise prescription. The Rockport Fitness Walking Test is an easy way to determine your present level of conditioning. All you have to do is walk a mile. You then follow a program specially designed for your needs. For a free copy, send an SASE [self-addressed stamped envelope] to: The Rockport Walking Institute, P.O. Box 480, Marlboro, MA 01752.

5. Write it down. You may be accustomed to scheduling your workday on a calendar. Do the same with exercise.

6. Start easy. Studies show muscle soreness peaks in 24 to 48 hours, so don't plunge into unfamiliar movements that leave you aching. But realize that some soreness is natural—it happens to the best of us.

7. Vary activities. This is especially important during the change of seasons. If you're a fair-weather exerciser, plan ahead for activities you can do indoors during the winter. Variety will also help prevent injuries and boredom.

8. Go for low injury potential. Walking and stationary cycling are safe, low-impact sports. Injuries are the death knell of exercise programs.

9. Consider past injuries. Here's another reason for choosing low-injury activities. A Stanford University program found that many people who started running soon quit because of knee problems. Though the exercisers blamed running, the researchers discovered that most of them had bum knees before they started.

10. Choose a health club devoted to long-term health. While most clubs today no longer practice the once-common method of taking your dues and hoping you don't use the space, some are more responsible than others. Two national organizations that represent quality clubs are the YMCA of the U.S.A. and the International Racquet Sports Association (IRSA).

11. Consider other habits—it may be time for a lifestyle change. If you smoke, the chances of staying with exercise are much lower. But if you keep exercising, the chances of giving up tobacco rise rapidly. Also, *American Health*'s Gallup studies show that people who get into exercise begin to eat more fruit and vegetables and make other healthy changes.

12 Choose exercise you enjoy. Don't run if you don't like it. Try walking or biking instead. If you hate the feel of sweat, consider swimming.

13. Opt for quality equipment. Nothing will steer you away from exercise faster than an uncomfortable bike seat or weight equipment that doesn't move smoothly. Check the club you're considering joining to see whether it has well-maintained quality equipment.

14. Be aware of the transition out of school. Many high school and college athletes never make the move from intense, frequent conditioning for a sport to lifelong fitness maintenance. It's time to think about the long run, not the next victory. And you get spoiled at school: You won't always have easy access to facilities and dozens of friends to work out with.

15. Use a health club that's convenient to your schedule. It's not necessarily convenience of location that's important: Most exercisers will go a little out of their way for a quality facility. But it's discouraging if you can only exercise at 8 a.m., when everyone's fighting for the rowing machines.

16. Avoid exercising at high intensity. Studies by Michael Pollock, exercise physiologist at the University of Florida College of Medicine, found that people exercising hard (90% of their maximum heart rate reserve, the difference between resting and maximum heart rate) had a 50% chance of getting injured during a 20-week program, while those who followed a more moderate walking and jogging program had only a 20% risk.

17. Use your heavy workload as the reason to exercise. "I'm too busy" isn't an adequate excuse. I surveyed 1,100 CEOS last year and found that people who worked the most were most likely to exercise.

18. Exercise with, or simply support, other family members or friends. Long-term adherence to exercise improves when a woman stands by her man—and vice versa.

19. Give yourself frequent self-tests. We tend to notice the bad things (sore muscles), but not the good. After exercise, ask yourself: Do I feel less tired? Am I in a better mood? If your body and mind tell you the benefits are already there, you're on the way to the next workout.

20. Remember the long-term benefits. If you stay with exercise for 20 weeks, it's very likely you'll exercise throughout your life. Reason: You'll see improvements in self-esteem. Exercise then becomes even more self-reinforcing. And research has shown that once you've exercised this long, even if you quit for a while, you'll probably return to it again.

21. Take lessons. You'll reap benefits immediately with activities like walking, but other more complicated activities pose a problem and may not be aerobic if done incorrectly. You need instruction to learn to swim the crawl properly or you'll end up wasting time—and energy—struggling in the water. Improper technique on a rowing machine can simply cause sore arms and frustration.

22. Opt for motivational equipment. Technology now being applied to fitness equipment emphasizes motivation as much as enhanced performance. Fun equipment—such as a stationary cycle with a computerized hill profile—keeps people coming back for more.

23. Follow the 2% rule. People often increase exercise too rapidly. You don't want to add a 10-lb. weight plate every week on the barbell. Stick to a 2% weekly increase as your goal. If you walk one mile the first week, don't plan to walk two miles the next week. That's a 100% increase—and an invitation for soreness and injury.

24. Keep weight-loss goals modest. I recommend trying to lose 1 lb. a week.

25. Join a class. Beginners benefit greatly not only from the instruction but also from the social setting of the class.

26. Get a dog. Rover needs frequent walking, doesn't he? Per Olaf Astrand, the frontier exercise physiologist from Sweden, observed that Americans cared more about the health of their pets than themselves. Those r[...] man's best friend will also help [...] the leash.

27. Keep exercise time around 30 [...] less a session. Studies by Dr. Pollock [...] difference in aerobic benefits between [...] utes and 45 minutes of exercise, but the nu[...] of injuries increased dramatically at 45 minu[...]

28. Deal with the boredom before it come[s] up. After 20 weeks, the beneficial reinforcements of exercise should kick in, so plan variations (trying different exercise, using motivational equipment, etc.) early in your exercise program.

29. Exercise to eat. Working out offers one of the few remaining excuses to eat more, to indulge occasionally without guilt. In a world where we're always told to stop, eating and exercise are two things you can give yourself.

Source: James M. Rippe, M.D., *American Health* (June 1988), pp. 43–46.

For some people, making exercise a part of their lives is a change that requires considerable discipline and planning. For others, it is an easy adjustment.

At the outset of a new fitness program, enthusiasm is usually high and the sense of resolve unshakable. Nevertheless, upon settling in to the routine, many people find their dedication waning. What often follows is inconsistent participation, then lack of visible progress, and finally discouragement. Indeed, about 50 percent of people who begin an exercise program drop out within the first 6 months. [7]

Nearly everyone will experience setbacks along the road to fitness. Setbacks come in many forms. Common ones include (but certainly are not limited to) a sickness such as a cold or flu, a spate of bad weather, a busy holiday season, and a heavy study or work period. Clearly, the list of potential distractions is endless. Each of us can think of things in our lives that could tempt us to pass up an exercise session. Therefore, it is imperative to develop strategies to overcome them.

FIGURE 6.6
nal Commitment Form

COMMITMENT FORM

_____

_____

_____

_____

...gin my program on _____.

I will maintain a weekly record of my activities.

Date	Day	Warm-up	Activity	Heart Rate	Cool-down	Comments
	Sunday					
	Monday					
	Tuesday					
	Wednesday					
	Thursday					
	Friday					
	Saturday					

_____   _____
signature   date

Keeping a record of when and how much you exercise gives you a chance to document your progress and to remind yourself of your goals.

Adhering to Your Program

The mechanisms that underlie successful adherence to exercise programs are not completely understood. [8] However, several helpful strategies have been identified. The most critical element is for you to follow a training program that meets your individual needs and abilities. This will help to keep your interest high, since you will begin to see the results of your efforts.

In choosing a health club, your individual fitness goals and objectives should be your guide. To what extent can the club support those goals? Does the club provide the activities that you find most enjoyable? Is there a good variety of equipment (cardiovascular as well as weight machines, etc.)? Some points to consider are:

Beware of overcrowding: Visit the club during the hours that you expect to be using it. Are there long waits for each machine? Does the space seem too crowded? Does the club limit its membership size to prevent this?

Choosing a Health Club

Cleanliness and maintenance: Are the workout spaces and the locker rooms clean? Is most of the equipment well-maintained and operable, or are several pieces out of order?

Location: Is the club's location convenient for you?

Health screening: Most reputable clubs provide some form of health screening for their clients. Are optional fitness tests offered?

Staffing: What types of qualifications are staff members required to have? Many centers hire only personnel with degrees in exercise science or related fields. Certifications are also required in many facilities. Several certifying agencies exist, so it is important to look for the most well-established, such as the American College of Sports Medicine, the Institute for Aerobics Research, the National Strength and Conditioning Association, and the International Dance/Exercise Association.

Consultation and supervision: Do members receive individualized fitness consultation as part of the club's service? Are the weight rooms adequately supervised with trained staff?

Membership fees and contracts: Are the fees reasonable as compared to other clubs in the area? Does the contract contain everything that may have been promised orally? Is membership transferable?

Did You Know That . . .

Personal fitness trainers who design individual fitness programs charge between $20 and $100 an hour for guided exercise sessions.

Creating a formal commitment to the training program by completing a written "contract" such as the one shown in Figure 6.6 is often advisable. Asking for the support or participation of a family member or friend can be of great value, if only because it commits you publicly to your goal.

Fitness specialists often suggest keeping a training journal. Such record-keeping helps to keep you on track, document your progress, and avoid overtraining.

Finally, avoid boredom. Try new activities. If you have access to a swimming pool, for example, try an aqua-aerobics class, underwater stretches and strengthening exercises, and lap-swim-ming. Exercise in a variety of different sites—in your home, at a local park, and, if possible, at a health club or gym. Varying your exercise routine in these and other ways will allow you to expand your choices and sustain your interest.

We encourage you not to view physical fitness as a static state. Rather, envision your pursuit of fitness as a dynamic, lifelong process of wellness. You will experience many health-promoting and life-style-enhancing benefits as a result of becoming a dedicated, committed exerciser. W

Glossary

A

Aerobic: Having to do with oxygen. Aerobic exercise is exercise designed to produce a sustained increase in heart rate and whose energy costs can be met by the body from aerobic sources, i.e., from increased oxygen consumption.

Anorexia nervosa: A psychological and physiological condition characterized by a refusal or inability to eat, leading to severe weight loss, malnutrition, hormonal imbalance, and other potentially life-threatening changes.

Antagonistic muscle: The muscle that produces the opposite joint action to that of the prime mover or active muscle.

Atherosclerosis: A form of hardening of the arteries (arteriosclerosis) in which a substance known as plaque gradually accumulates on the interior of the artery walls, narrowing the arteries and reducing their elasticity.

B

Body composition: The relative percentages of fat and fat-free mass.

Bulimia: A psychological and physiological condition characterized by recurrent episodes of binge eating, usually followed by self-induced vomiting, use of laxatives or diuretics, or vigorous exercise in order to prevent weight gain.

C

Calorie: The amount of heat energy required to raise the temperature of 1 gram of water 1 degree centigrade. The calories used in measuring the energy value of food are equivalent to 1,000 of these "small calories" and are, therefore, technically kilocalories (kcal), although in common usage we refer to them simply as calories.

Cardiovascular disease (CVD): Any of several forms of disease of the heart and blood vessels.

Cardiovascular fitness: The ability of the heart and blood vessels to supply fuel, especially oxygen, to the muscles during continuous activity, and the ability of the muscles to take up and utilize the oxygen that is delivered. Also called aerobic fitness.

Cardiovascular system: The heart and blood vessels; the circulatory system.

Cholesterol: A fatlike substance found in food derived from animals and also manufactured by the body. It is essential to nerve and brain cell function, the synthesis of sex hormones, and is a component of bile acids used to aid fat digestion. Cholesterol is also part of the plaque that accumulates on artery walls as a result of atherosclerosis.

Circuit training: A form of weight training in which participants complete lifting exercises in rapid succession at various stations comprising a "circuit;" particularly suited to increasing muscular endurance, circuit training may also be used to increase muscular strength.

Compression: Wrapping an injured area with an elastic bandage or similar device immediately following injury, in an attempt to minimize swelling.

Conduction: A thermoregulatory process by which heat is transferred from a warmer to a cooler object when the two come in contact.

Convection: The transfer of heat from a warmer to a cooler portion of a fluid or gas as a result of a current or movement, as when heat generated in the muscles during exercise is transferred to the surface of the body by the movement of the blood.

Cool-down: The concluding phase of a workout or exercise session during which the body gradually returns to near pre-exercise conditions; walking until heart rate and respiration return to near normal is an example of a cool-down activity.

Core temperature: The body's internal temperature, normally maintained at about 37 degrees centigrade (98.6 degrees Fahrenheit).

Coronary arteries: The arteries that supply blood to the heart muscle.

Coronary heart disease: Temporary or permanent damage to the heart muscle resulting from an insufficient flow of blood through the coronary arteries.

D

Dehydration: A reduction in body fluid level (including blood volume) resulting from a failure to maintain fluid intake at a level sufficient to replace fluids lost through sweating and other thermoregulatory mechanisms; the early signs of dehydration include lethargy, anxiety, and irritability; severe dehydration can result in a loss of coordination and unconsciousness.

Diastolic blood pressure: The blood pressure level in the arteries during the filling phase of the heartbeat, reflected in the second, or lower, number of the blood pressure reading.

E

Electrolyte: A substance such as sodium, calcium, magnesium, or potassium, which is normally present in the body and carries an electrical charge (either positive or negative) when in solution. A correct balance of electrolytes is necessary for proper cell function.

Essential fat: Fat contained in various organs and portions of the nervous system that is essential to normal physiological functioning.

Evaporation: The process by which a liquid is converted to a gas, giving up heat in the process; the evaporation of perspiration from the surface of the skin is one of the body's natural thermoregulatory mechanisms.

Exercise: Physical activity performed in order to improve or maintain one's fitness and/or increase caloric consumption.

Exercise session: The time period within which a complete set of exercises is completed; each session consists of 3 phases—warm-up, main stimulus activity, and cool-down.

F

Fitness: The ability to meet the demands of daily living with energy to spare; possessing the functional capacity to do not only those tasks that are required, but also those activities that one enjoys.

Flexibility: The range of motion available at a joint or combination of joints.

Free weights: Weights such as dumbbells and barbells that are unattached to any larger piece of apparatus and are used in weight lifting.

G

Glycogen: A form of complex carbohydrate stored in the body, primarily in the liver and muscle tissue.

Graded exercise testing: Testing to determine exercise capacity during continuous cardiovascular work; usually performed on a treadmill or stationary cycle, it involves gradually increasing the amount of work performed until the individual reaches his or her VO_2 max; sometimes abbreviated as GXT.

H

High density lipoprotein (HDL) cholesterol: A form of lipoprotein that transports cholesterol and triglycerides in the blood; HDL cholesterol is the so-called "good cholesterol" that removes LDL cholesterol from the blood; high levels of HDL cholesterol are associated with a reduced risk of heart disease.

Hypertension: Chronically high blood pressure that exceeds the level thought to be healthful.

Hyperthermia: A condition characterized by an excessively high body temperature. Hyperthermia may be accompanied by the symptoms of heat exhaustion or heatstroke.

Hypothermia: A condition characterized by a subnormal body temperature. The symptoms of hypothermia include drowsiness and significantly reduced respiratory and heart rates.

I

Interval training: Alternating repetitions of higher-intensity exercise interspersed with lower-intensity but still active "recovery periods." Increases VO_2 max and thus cardiovascular fitness.

Isokinetic exercise: Strength training in which there is an attempt to move the joint or limb involved at a constant velocity.

Isometric exercise: Strength training involving the application of force against an immovable object (such as a wall or heavy weight); in isometric exercise there is little or no change in the length of the muscle.

Isotonic exercise: Strength training involving a fixed resistance that can be overcome by the muscle, resulting in the movement of the muscle and changes in its length; also called dynamic exercise.

L

Life-style: A way of living that consistently reflects a particular set of values and attitudes.

Lipoproteins: A class of proteins found in the blood that consist of a simple protein combined with a lipid (a fatty substance that is insoluble in the blood). They are transported throughout the body by the blood and are one of the body's important sources of food energy.

Low density lipoprotein (LDL) cholesterol: A form of lipoprotein that transports cholesterol and triglycerides in the blood; LDL cholesterol is the so-called "bad cholesterol" that forms deposits on the interior walls of the arteries; high levels of LDL cholesterol are associated with an increased risk of heart disease.

M

Maximum heart rate reserve: The range between an individual's resting and maximum heart rates; the target heart rate for any given individual and set of exercises will fall within this range.

Muscular endurance: The ability of a muscle or group of muscles to sustain a given level of force.

Muscular strength: The ability of a muscle or group of muscles to exert a maximal amount of force.

Myocardial infarction: The sudden death of a portion of the heart muscle; a heart attack.

O

Obesity: An excessive accumulation of body fat.

One repetition maximum (1RM): The maximum weight a person can move through the range of motion for one repetition of a particular exercise.

Osteoporosis: A chronic disturbance of bone metabolism in which the bone mass decreases and the bones become more fragile; the incidence of osteoporosis increases with age and is greater among women than men.

Overtraining: A term synonymous with exercising at an excessive level of intensity, frequency, or duration, which often leads to injury, pain, or excessive fatigue.

Overweight: A somewhat elusive term that is usually used to describe individuals whose body weight exceeds by at least 20 percent the maximum amount recommended for their age, sex, height, and build in insurance company actuarial tables.

P

Percentage of body fat: The percent of total body weight that is composed of fat; the ratio of the weight of *total body fat* to the weight of the *fat-free mass*.

Plaque: Fatty deposits that accumulate on arterial walls, restricting blood flow.

Principle of specificity: A basic training principle which states that the benefits derived from training are specific to the mode of activity.

R

R.I.C.E. principle: Rest, ice, compression, and elevation. The purpose of this treatment is to reduce pain, decrease swelling, and limit the amount of inflammation induced by an injury.

Radiation: A thermoregulatory process by which heat is transferred from a warmer to a cooler area even in the absence of direct physical contact; heat may be radiated away from the body, for example, when the temperature of the surrounding air is cooler than that of the body.

Resting metabolic rate: The rate of energy consumption necessary to maintain the body and perform vital body functions (breathing, heartbeat, maintenance of body temperature, etc.) at rest; increases in activity level result in corresponding increases in the metabolic rate.

S

Sedentary: Accustomed to being physically inactive.

Spot reduction myth: The unfounded belief that exercising specific portions of the body will result in the loss of subcutaneous storage fat in those areas.

Stations: The term used to identify the exercise activities that together comprise a circuit training program, e.g., a squat or bench press;

circuit training exercises may involve either free weights or weight machines.

Sticking point: The point at which the weight being moved is greater than the muscle's ability to move it.

Storage fat: Fat in excess of the body's immediate energy needs that accumulates in layers beneath the skin and within and around various organs of the body.

Systolic blood pressure: The blood pressure level in the arteries during the pumping phase of the heartbeat, reflected in the first, or higher, number of the blood pressure reading.

T

Thermoregulatory: Refers to the body's heat-regulating processes, which maintain the body's core temperature at the level needed for proper metabolic functioning.

Training: A program of regular exercise of a frequency, intensity, and duration sufficient to produce a measurable improvement in one or more fitness components.

Training effect: Measurable physiological changes resulting from a program of regular exercise incorporating appropriate frequency, intensity, and duration for the individual's needs.

Triglycerides: Fatty compounds found in foods and made in the body, consisting of a carbon "backbone" to which are attached 3 fatty acids.

V

VO_2 max: The maximum quantity of oxygen that can be delivered to and consumed by the organs of the body at any given time; also known as maximum oxygen uptake, VO_2 max is usually measured as either liters of oxygen (O_2) consumed per minute (absolute VO_2 max) or as liters of oxygen consumed per minute divided by body weight in kilograms (relative VO_2 max).

W

Warm-up: The initial phase of a workout or exercise session whose purpose is to prepare the body for more strenuous activity; typical warm-up activities include slow jogging, light stretching, or a low-intensity "rehearsal" of the activity to follow.

Wellness: An approach to personal health that emphasizes the importance of a variety of behaviors in promoting health and preventing disease.

Notes

Chapter 1

1. Jon Feld, "Sports Survey," *Club Industry*, (August 1988): 20–22.
2. A. Donald Anderson, "What's New in the Fitness Business," *New York Times*, 3 January 1988, C13.
3. "Protective Effect of Physical Activity on Coronary Heart Disease," *Mortality and Morbidity Weekly Report* 36, no. 26 (10 July 1987): 428.
4. American Heart Association, *Heart and Stroke Facts 1991* (Dallas: American Heart Association, 1991), 1.
5. American Heart Association, p. 11.
6. R. Sannerstedt, "Hypertension," in *Exercise Testing and Exercise Prescription for Special Cases*, J. S. Skinner, ed. (Philadelphia: Lea & Febiger, 1987).
7. American Heart Association, p. 2.
8. One of the very first such studies, now viewed as a landmark in the field, is W. F. Enos, R. H. Holmes, and J. Beyer, "Coronary Disease Among U.S. Soldiers Killed in Action in Korea," *Journal of the American Medical Association* 152 (1953): 1090–1093.
9. National Institutes of Health Consensus Development Conference statement, *Health Implications of Obesity*, vol. 5 (Washington, DC: U.S. Government Printing Office, 1985).
10. K. D. Brownell, "Obesity and Weight Control: The Good and Bad of Dieting," *Nutrition Today* 3 (1987): 4–9.
11. J. H. Wilmore and David L. Costill, *Training for Sport and Activity: The Physiological Basis of the Conditioning Process* 3d ed. (Dubuque: William C. Brown, 1989).
12. R. R. Cottrell, *Wellness: Weight Control*, (Guilford, CT: Dushkin Publishing Group, 1991), 16–17.
13. A. J. Rampone and P. J. Reynolds, "Obesity: Thermodynamic Principles in Perspective," *Life Sciences* 43 (1989): 93–110.
14. Wilmore and Costill.
15. M. J. Pollock and J. H. Wilmore, *Exercise in Health and Disease: Evaluation & Rehabilitation* 2d ed. (Philadelphia: W. B. Saunders, 1990).
16. See, for example, A. S. Jackson, M. J. Pollock, and A. Ward, "Generalized Equations for Predicting Body Density of Women," *Medicine and Science in Sport and Exercise* 12 (1980): 175–182, and A. S. Jackson and M. J. Pollock, "Generalized Equations for Predicting Body Density of Men," *British Journal of Nutrition* 40 (1983): 497–504.

Chapter 2

1. American College of Sports Medicine, *Guidelines for Exercise Testing and Prescription* 4th ed. (Philadelphia: Lea & Febiger, 1991), 35.
2. E. L. Fox, T. E. Kirby, and A. R. Fox, *Bases of Fitness* (New York: Macmillan, 1987).
3. American College of Sports Medicine, 4th ed., p. 9.
4. B. Saltin and P. D. Gollnick, "Skeletal Muscle Adaptability: Significance for Metabolism and Performance," chapter 9 in *Handbook of Physiology*, L. D. Peachey, R. H. Adrian, and S. R. Geiger, eds., (Baltimore: Williams and Wilkins, 1983).
5. W. D. McArdle, F. I. Katch, and V. L. Katch, *Exercise Physiology: Energy, Nutrition, and Human Performance*, 2d ed. (Philadelphia: Lea & Febiger, 1986).
6. V. P. Lombardi, *Beginning Weight Training* (Dubuque, IA: William C. Brown, 1989), 43.
7. R. Hettinger, *Physiology of Strength* (Springfield, IL: Charles C. Thomas, 1961); S. J. Fleck and R. C. Schutt, "Types of Strength Training," *Clinics in Sports Medicine* 4 (1985): 159–168.
8. Lombardi, p. 54.
9. W. Westcott, *Strength Fitness: Physiological Principles and Training Techniques* 3d ed. (Dubuque, IA: William C. Brown, 1991), 105, 108.
10. Saltin and Gollnick.
11. American College of Sports Medicine, 4th ed., p. 111.
12. M. A. Moore and R. S. Hutton, "Electromyographic Investigation of Muscle Stretching Techniques," *Medicine and Science in Sport and Exercise* 5 (1980): 322–329; W. E. Prentice, "A Comparison of Static Stretching and PNF Stretching for Improving Hip Joint Flexibility," *Athletic Training* 1 (1983): 56–59.
13. But some experts argue that strength training is at least as effective as or possibly preferable to aerobic or cardiovascular training as a means of altering body composition. See, for example, Wescott, p. 74.

Chapter 3

1. R. J. Shepard, "Physiological Changes Over the Years," in American College of Sports Medicine, *Manual for Guidelines for Exercise Testing and Prescription* (Philadelphia: Lea & Febiger, 1988), 297–304.

2. American Heart Association, p. 11.

3. American Heart Association, *About High Blood Pressure* (Dallas: American Heart Association, 1989).

4. D. R. Seals and J. M. Hagberg, "The Effect of Training on Human Hypertension," *Medicine and Science in Sport and Exercise* 16 (1984): 207–215

5. C. M. Tipton, "Exercise Training and Hypertension," in *Exercise and Sport Science Reviews* 12, Ronald L. Terjung, ed., (Lexington, MA: D. C. Heath, 1984): 245–306.

6. Tipton.

7. W. L. Haskell, "The Influence of Exercise on the Concentration of Triglyceride and Cholesterol in Human Plasma," in *Exercise and Sport Science Reviews* 16, Kent B. Pandolf, ed., (New York: Macmillan, 1988).

8. Seals and Hagberg.

9. W. P. Castelli et al., "HDL Cholesterol and Other Lipids in Coronary Heart Disease," *Circulation* 55 (1977): 76–77; P. Clarkson et al., "High-density Lipoprotein Cholesterol in Young Adult Weight Lifters, Runners, and Untrained Subjects," *Human Biology* 53 (1981): 251–257; Z. V. Tran et al., "The Effects of Exercise on Blood Lipids and Lipoproteins: A Meta-analysis," *Medicine and Science in Sport and Exercise* 15 (1983): 393–402.

10. T. C. Rotkis et al., "Relationship Between High-density Lipoprotein Cholesterol and Weekly Running Mileage," *Journal of Cardiac Rehabilitation* 2 (1982): 109–112.

11. Hurley et al., "Resistive Training Can Reduce Coronary Risk Factors Without Altering VO$_2$ Max or Percent Body Fat, *Medicine and Science in Sport and Exercise* 2: 150–154.

12. A. Berg, G. Ringwald, and J. Keul, "Lipoprotein Cholesterol and Well-trained Athletes," *International Journal of Sports Medicine* 1 (1980): 137–138.

13. L. C. Lipson et al., "Effect of Exercise Training on High-density Lipoproteins and Other Lipoproteins," *Atherosclerosis* 37 (1980): 529–538.

14. K. D. Brownell, "Obesity and Weight Control: The Good and Bad of Dieting," *Nutrition Today* 3 (1987): 4–9.

15. Brownell.

16. P. Webb, "Direct Calorimetry and the Energetics of Exercise and Weight Loss," *Medicine and Science in Sport and Exercise* 1 (1985): 3–7.

17. B. A. McPherson, "Psychological Effects of an Exercise Program for Post-infarct and Normal Adult Men," *Journal of Sports Medicine and Fitness* 7 (1967): 61–66.

18. B. D. Hatfield and D. M. Landers, "Psychophysiology in

Exercise and Sport Research: An Overview," in *Exercise and Sport Science Reviews* (New York: Macmillan, 1987).

19. H. A. DeVries et al., "Tranquilizer Effect of Exercise," *American Journal of Physical Medicine* 60 (1981): 57–66.

20. A. H. Ismail and P. J. Young, "The Effect of Chronic Exercise on the Personality of Middle-Aged Men by Univariate and Multivariate Approaches," *Journal of Human Ergonomics* 2 (1976): 45–57.

21. S. F. Siconolfi et al., "Exercise Training Attenuated the Blood Pressure Response to Mental Stress," *Medicine and Science in Sport and Exercise* 17 (1985): 281.

22. C. H. Folkins, S. Lynch, and M. M. Gardner, "Psychological Fitness as a Function of Physical Fitness," *Archives of Physical Medicine and Rehabilitation* 53 (1972): 503–508; National Institute of Mental Health, *Consensus Statement on Exercise and Mental Health* (Washington DC: U.S. Government Printing Office, 1987).

Chapter 4

1. P. O. Astrand and K. Rodahl, *Textbook of Work Physiology,* 3d ed. (New York: McGraw-Hill, 1986), 584–589.

2. J. A. Vogel, B. H. Jones, and P. Rock, "Environmental Considerations in Exercise Testing and Training," in *Guidelines for Exercise Testing and Prescription*, American College of Sports Medicine (Philadelphia: Lea & Febiger, 1989), 90–91.

3. Wilmore and Costill, pp. 264–276.

4. Vogel, Jones, and Rock.

5. M. H. Ellestad, *Stress Testing: Principles and Practice* (Philadelphia: F. A. Davis, 1986), 118–120.

6. Pollock and Wilmore, pp. 628–630.

7. Pollock and Wilmore, 628–630.

8. B. H. Jones, P. Rock, and M. P. Moore, "Musculoskeletal Injuries: Risks, Prevention, and First Aid," in *Resource Manual for Exercise Testing and Prescription*, American College of Sports Medicine (Philadelphia: Lea & Febiger, 1989), 285–295.

Chapter 5

1. American College of Sports Medicine, 4th ed., pp. 95–102.

2. Wilmore and Costill, pp. 167–171.

3. American College of Sports Medicine, 4th ed., pp. 95–96.

4. American College of Sports Medicine, 4th ed., p. 96.

5. G. Borg, "Perceived Exertion as an Indicator of Somatic Stress," *Scandinavian Journal of Rehabilitative Medicine* 2 (1970): 92–98.

6. E. F. Coyle et al., "Time Course of Loss of Adaptations After Stopping Prolonged Intense Endurance Training," *Journal of Applied Physiology* 57 (1984): 1857–1864.

7. S. J. Fleck and W. J. Kraemer, *Designing Resistance Training Programs* (Champaign, IL.: Human Kinetics, 1987), 5–20.

8. C. B. Corbin and L. Noble, "Flexibility: A Major Component of Physical Fitness," *Journal of Physical Education and Recreation* 6 (1980): 24–25, 57–60.

Chapter 6

1. American College of Sports Medicine, *Guidelines for Exercise Testing and Prescription.*

2. British Columbia Ministry of Health, *Physical Activity Readiness Questionnaire Validation Report* (Vancouver, British Columbia: Department of National Health and Welfare, 1975).

3. McArdle, Katch, and Katch, p. 434.

4. McArdle, Katch, and Katch, p. 438.

5. McArdle, Katch, and Katch, p. 439.

6. U.S. Department of Health and Human Services, *Morbidity and Mortality Weekly Report* 11 (1989): 448–452.

7. R. K. Dishman, "Health Psychology and Exercise Adherence," *Quest* 3 (1982): 168.

8. *See* R. K. Dishman, *Exercise Adherence, Its Impact on Public Health* (Champaign, Ill.: Human Kinetics, 1988).

Resources

BOOKS

Anderson, Bob. *Stretching*. New York: Random House, 1980.

This useful book shows the correct way to stretch for fitness and muscle flexibility. More than 200 stretches and stretching routines for 36 different sports and activities are illustrated with over 1,000 drawings.

Bouchard, Claude, et al., eds. *Exercise, Fitness, and Health: A Consensus of Current Knowledge*. Champaign, IL: Human Kinetics, 1990.

This book provides a review of current knowledge about the relationships among exercise, fitness, and health. Eighty-seven scientists present 62 papers that examine the cardiovascular implications of fitness and exercise. A broad range of topics is addressed, including the relationships of exercise, fitness, and health to physiology, genetics, psychology, anthropology, anatomy, immunology, nutrition, and more.

Burstein, Nancy. *Soft Aerobics: The New Low-Impact Workout*. New York: Putnam, 1987.

This book presents an alternative to traditional, high-impact aerobics (which can cause injury from excess stress on ankles, shins, calves, knees, hips, and back). It offers 12 low-impact exercises combined into 4 different exercise routines and is illustrated with step-by-step photographs. Readers can follow the specific routines presented in the book or create a personalized program for individual fitness levels. The program is effective for losing weight as well as for preventing osteoporosis in women.

Clark, Nancy. *Nancy Clark's Sports Nutrition Guidebook*. Champaign, IL: Human Kinetics, 1990.

The author provides information to help athletic people create diets for high energy and for lifelong nutrition. Clark presents over 100 easy-to-prepare recipes, with accompanying nutrition content information for each recipe. This book is useful not only to devoted athletes, Olympians, and fitness professionals but also to the moderate exerciser as well.

Constable, George, ed. *Super Firm: Tough Work-outs*. New York: Time-Life Books, 1989.

Chapters contain information on exercise without weights; myths about power eating; getting the most from calisthenics; and techniques for increasing strength, endurance, and flexibility. The muscle groups are explained as well as how to target each one and how to develop a personal exercise course.

Constable, George, ed. *Walking and Running: The Complete Guide*. New York: Time-Life Books, 1989.

This book discusses the health and fitness benefits of walking and running, how they compare as aerobic conditioners, how to minimize the chance of injury, how to select the right shoes, and how to eat right for an exercise lifestyle. Also covered are tips on coping with heat and cold, maintaining the most efficient stride, and muscle strengthening.

Cooper, Kenneth H., M.D. *Running Without Fear: How to Reduce the Risk of Heart Attack and Sudden Death During Aerobic Exercise*. New York: M. Evans and Company, 1985.

Dr. Cooper provides sensible guidelines to show that too much exercise does not lead to better health and, in fact, may be dangerous, and gives encouragement for those who are afraid to start running. The author describes proper cool-down after long-distance running and how, when, and where sudden death is most likely to strike. He also provides information on reducing cardiovascular disease and discusses how all forms of exercise, whether running, swimming, bicycling, skiing, or aerobic dancing, can help control stress for better health.

Franks, B. Don, and Edward T. Howley. *Fitness Facts: The Healthy Living Handbook*. Champaign, IL: Human Kinetics, 1989.

This book discusses how to test fitness, improve fitness level, and set up an individual fitness program. Using current research, the authors answer many basic questions about exercise and fitness. Chapters contain fitness progress self-evaluation, definitions of fitness, how to change to more healthful behaviors, selecting the right fitness program, injury prevention, and more.

Guide to More Healthful Living. Edited by the Blue Cross Association. New York: Contemporary Books, 1986.

This book covers overall wellness of body and mind. Written and compiled by 9 medical doctors, chapter titles include Wellness, Nutrition, Physical Fitness, Reducing Stress, and Your Health and Fitness Life-style. Two additional sections include Your Healthy Best Score Card, which allows you to chart your health progress, and The Life Management Self-Evaluation Test, which includes questions about eating habits, physical activity, environment, smoking habits, and stress evaluations, all culminating in your own total Life Management score.

Kingsbury, Bonnie D. *Full Figure Fitness: A Program for Teaching Overweight Adults.* Champaign, IL: Human Kinetics, 1988.

A quality exercise program for fitness instructors and exercise specialists to use with overweight adults. This book helps obese adults understand the complex nature of obesity and offers practical advice from experts in psychology, physical therapy, and nutrition. Kingsbury based this book on her many years of teaching fitness classes to overweight adults. Provided also is marketing and promotional information for fitness instructors to set up a Full Figure Fitness program. The book is also useful to individuals who want to know more about appropriate exercise programs for the overweight adult.

Meyers, Casey. *Aerobic Walking: The Best and Safest Weight Loss and Cardiovascular Exercise for Everyone Overweight or Out of Shape.* New York: Random House, 1987.

This book addresses the benefits of walking for the purpose of disease prevention and helping with weight control problems. Topics covered include the proper walking gaits for maximum aerobic benefits and reduced stress on joints and how to develop a self-tailored fitness walking program.

Sharkey, Brian J. *Physiology of Fitness* (3d ed.). Champaign, IL: Human Kinetics, 1990.

This book is easy to understand and use and provides important information about aerobic fitness, muscular fitness, energy balance, weight control, and the psychology of being physically fit. The author provides a thorough explanation of how fitness is achieved and maintained and explains why and how the body responds to regular exercise.

The Stanford Health and Exercise Handbook. Stanford Alumni Association Staff. Champaign, IL: Human Kinetics, 1987.

This book was created to accompany the Stanford Health and Exercise Program video listed under the videotape section later in this appendix. The book is designed to help individuals assess their own fitness levels, set up personal fitness regimens, and maintain these programs for a lifetime. It is written in everyday language that makes clear to readers the major health benefits of exercise: improved cardiovascular health, weight control, reduced serum cholesterol, lowered blood sugar, lowered blood pressure, increased bone density, psychological enhancement, and greater longevity.

Wilmore, Jack H. *Sensible Fitness* (2d ed.). Champaign, IL: Human Kinetics, 1986.

The author provides safe and sound guidelines for exercising and developing a healthy lifestyle. Information is provided on building strength, flexibility, and muscular endurance; weight control; nutrition; motivation; and injury prevention.

NEWSLETTERS

Consumer Reports Health Letter is published monthly by Consumers Union of the United States, a nonprofit organization that provides information and advice on goods, services, health, and personal finance. A one-year subscription is $24, and one for 2 years costs $38. Write to the Subscription Director, Consumer Reports Health Letter, Box 56356, Boulder, CO 80322-6356, or call (800) 274-8370.

Harvard Health Letter is published monthly as a nonprofit service by the Department of Continuing Education, Harvard Medical School, in association with Harvard University Press. The letter has the goal of interpreting health information for general readers in a timely and accurate fashion. A one-year subscription is $21. Write to the Harvard Medical School Letter, 79 Garden Street, Cambridge, MA 02138, or call customer service at (617) 495-3975.

Healthline is published monthly by Healthline Publishing, Inc. The letter is intended to educate readers about ways to help themselves avoid illness and live longer, healthier lives. A one-year subscription is $19, or $34 for 2 years. Write to Healthline, The C. V. Mosby Company, 11830 Westline Industrial Drive, St. Louis, MO 63146-3318, or call (800) 325-4177 (ext. 351).

Lahey Clinic Health Letter is published monthly to bring readers timely, relevant information about important medical issues. Continuing topics include general healthfulness, natural and processed foods, depression, exercise, alcohol, prescription medicine therapy, major diseases, and exercise. A one-year subscription is $18. Write to the Lahey Clinic Health Letter, Subscription Department, P.O. Box 541, Burlington, MA 01805.

Mayo Clinic Nutrition Letter is published monthly and provides reliable information about nutrition and fitness and how decisions on these matters affect your health. A one-year subscription is $24. Write to the Mayo Foundation for Medical Education and Research, 200 1st Street SW, Rochester, MN 55905, or call (800) 888-3968.

Tufts University Diet and Nutrition Letter is published monthly and covers topics related to nutrition and wellness, including exercise, diet and disease, and food consumerism. A one-year subscription costs $20. Write to the Tufts University Diet and Nutrition Letter, 53 Park Place, New York, NY 10007.

University of California Berkeley Wellness Letter is published monthly and covers many topics, including nutrition, fitness, and stress management. A one-year subscription is $20. Write to the University of California Berkeley Wellness Letter, P.O. Box 420148, Palm Coast, FL 32142.

PERIODICALS

American Health Magazine: Fitness of Body and Mind is published 10 times a year and covers many aspects of physical and mental well-being. In addition to feature articles, ongoing departments include Nutrition News, Fitness Reports, Mind/Body News, Family Report, Family Pet, and more. A one-year subscription is $14.95. Write to American Health: Fitness of Body and Mind, P.O. Box 3015, Harlan, IA 51537-3015.

Current Health 2: The Continuing Guide to Health Education is published monthly from September through May. Each issue contains a fea-

ture article plus a number of shorter pieces on topics such as drugs, psychology, your personal health, disease, and nutrition. For subscription information, contact *Current Health 2*, Publication and Subscription Offices, Field Publications, 4343 Equity Drive, Columbus, Ohio 43228.

In Health Magazine is published 6 times a year and provides articles on a number of health issues. In addition to recipes and practical nutrition tips, the magazine regularly includes self-help resources for consumers. A one-year subscription is $18. Write to In Health, P.O. Box 52431, Boulder, CO 80321-2431.

Priorities: For Long Life & Good Health is published quarterly by the American Council of Science and Health, Inc., (ACSH), a nonprofit consumer education association concerned with nutrition, chemicals, life-style factors, the environment, and human health. General individual membership in ACSH, which includes a subscription to Priorities, costs $25 a year. Write to the Subscription Department, Priorities, 1995 Broadway, 16th Floor, New York, NY 10023-5860.

Running & FitNews is published monthly by the American Running and Fitness Association, a nonprofit educational association of athletes and sports medicine professionals. This newsletter provides information on exercise guidelines, injury prevention, diet, and health-related fitness topics. A one-year subscription is $25. Write to the AR&FA, 9310 Old Georgetown Road, Bethesda, MD 20814, or call (301) 897-0197.

HOTLINES

Institute for Aerobic Research, (800) 527-8362. This number will provide information on computer services, continuing education consultation, physiology, hypertension, nutrition, and stress management as they relate to exercise and fitness. Callers can also get information about women's health studies and youth fitness. A further explanation of this organization is provided under the Government, Consumer, and Advocacy Groups section of this appendix.

National Health Information Center, Department of Health and Human Services, (800) 336-4797. Operated by the Office of Disease Prevention and Health Promotion, this information and referral center's trained personnel will direct you to the organization or government agency that can assist you with your health questions, whether they're about high blood pressure, cancer, fitness, or any other topic. Available 9 A.M. to 5 P.M., Eastern Standard Time, Monday through Friday.

Tel-Med is a free telephone service provided in many cities. Callers may request specific tapes by number and have them played over the phone. There are over 300 medical topics to choose from, including topics related to maintaining a healthy life-style, and many states provide toll-free numbers for this service. For the number of your nearest Tel-Med office, call local information or write to Tel-Med, Box 970, Colton, CA 92324.

VIDEOTAPES

The following video program related to wellness topics can be ordered from the National Wellness Institute, Inc., South Hall, 1319 Fremont Street, Stevens Point, WI 54481. Write for format, price, and ordering information.

Stanford Health and Exercise Program brings together fitness specialists and world-class athletes to introduce the concepts and practical tools found in the accompanying handbook, *The Stanford Health and Exercise Handbook.* Among the topics covered are the 8 prime benefits of exercise, how to determine your basic level of fitness, the actual Stanford Workout program, and 3 low-impact aerobic workouts.

The next video is available from Nutrition Counseling and Education Services (NC&ES), P.O. Box 3018, Olathe, KS 66062-3018. Write for prices and ordering information, or call (913) 782-8230. The following toll-free number is for placing orders only: (800) 445-5653. All videos in VHS format only.

Fitness Walking Program explains how to set up your own walking program, including warm-up and cool-down exercises. An 80-page accompanying booklet is provided.

GOVERNMENT, CONSUMER, AND ADVOCACY GROUPS

American College of Sports Medicine (ACSM), P.O. Box 1440, Indianapolis, IN 46206, (317) 637-9200

This group seeks to advance and disseminate knowledge dealing with motivation, responses, adaptations, and the effects of sports and other motor activities on the health of human beings at various stages in their lives. The ACSM sponsors regional workshops, seminars, and lecture tours. The organization also maintains biographical archives and is affiliated with the President's Council on Physical Fitness and Sports.

American Running and Fitness Association (AR&FA), 9310 Old Georgetown Rd., Bethesda, MD 20814, (301) 897-0197

Founded in 1968, this association consists of individual runners, exercise enthusiasts, and sports medicine professionals. The AR&FA promotes running and other aerobic activities as a preventive approach to health maintenance. The organization collects data on running and fitness and stores this information in a 2,000-volume library that specializes in publications on preventive medicine through exercise. This group is responsible for publishing *Running and FitNews* monthly and *Successful Jogging: Tips for Beginning Runners.*

American Council of Science and Health (ACSH), 1995 Broadway, 16th Floor, New York, NY 10023, (212) 362-7044

The purpose of this council is to provide consumers with scientifically balanced evaluations of food, chemicals, the environment, and human health. Council personnel participate in government regulatory proceedings, public debates, and other forums, and write regularly for professional and scientific journals, popular magazines, and newspaper columns. The council also holds national press conferences and produces a self-syndicated series of health updates for radio; provides a 24-hour computer online service featuring articles, commentary, press releases, and questions and answers on health topics; and publishes brochures, pamphlets, and research reports on numerous health topics.

American Heart Association (AHA), 720 Greenville Avenue, Dallas, TX 75231, (214) 373-6300

The AHA supports research, education, and community service programs with the goal of reducing premature death and disability from stroke and cardiovascular disease. It publishes several books, periodicals, and pamphlets related to exercise and healthy heart management. State branches of the AHA can be located through directory information.

Association for Fitness in Business (AFB), 310 N. Alabama, Suite A100, Indianapolis, IN 46204, (317) 636-6621

Founded in 1974, this organization's members include fitness professionals employed by major companies that conduct fitness programs for employees. Students interested in the field of fitness instruction for businesses may also join. The AFB supports and assists in the development of quality programs of health and fitness and seeks to create an awareness of the importance of physical, emotional, and mental health among employees. The association encourages active research and serves as a clearinghouse on physical fitness. It produces several publications related to fitness and fitness training.

Association of Physical Fitness Centers (APFC), 600 Jefferson Street, Suite 202, Rockville, MD 20852, (301) 424-7744

Membership of the APFC includes owners and operators of 500 businesses or organizations promoting physical fitness by stressing exercise, training, and recreational and athletic activities. The association conducts research on health and physical fitness and provides educational and promotional information to help the fitness centers serve their customers. The APFC produces several publications, a periodic bulletin on legal issues concerning fitness centers, and a bimonthly fitness newsletter.

Fitness Motivation Institute of America Association (FMIAA), 36 Harold Avenue, San Jose, CA 95117, (408) 246-9191

This association is designed for persons professionally involved with health and physical fitness. The group seeks to motivate and educate individuals in the area of physical fitness. The FMIAA program is based on 4 parameters: why the body needs exercise, what a fit body is, methods of getting fit, and motivation to stay fit. Worldwide seminars are conducted regularly.

High Blood Pressure Information Center (HBPIC), 120/80 National Institutes of Health, Bethesda, MD 20205, (301) 652-7700

The HBPIC provides information on the detection, diagnosis, and management of high blood pressure to consumers and health professionals. The center identifies, collects, organizes, and disseminates information in many formats. Its sources are monographs, journals, newsletters, newspapers, reports, brochures, posters, and contracts with other health agencies and clearinghouses. It also provides reference and referral services, consultants, information on exercise programs for those who live with high blood pressure; it performs searches on the center's data base; and it recommends resources of other libraries and clearinghouses.

IDEA: The Association for Fitness Professionals, 6190 Cornerstone Court, E., Suite 204, San Diego, CA 92121, (619) 691-6299

IDEA serves as an educational network and forum for fitness instructors, program directors, personal trainers, exercise club and studio owners, and others in the fitness field. The group maintains a small library of books and magazines on physical fitness and conducts seminars and workshops. IDEA is affiliated with the American Heart Association. IDEA publishes the trade journal *IDEA Today* 10 times a year.

Institute for Aerobics Research (IAR), 12330 Preston Road, Dallas, TX 75230, (214) 701-8001

The goals of the IAR are to promote understanding of the relationship between life-style and health, to provide leadership in enhancing the physical and emotional well-being of individuals, and to encourage participation in aerobic exercise. Founded in 1970, the institute conducts innovative studies of health, living habits, and methods of implementing changes in living habits in order to develop a positive life-style. Publications include *Aerobics News,* monthly, and research findings in national and international medical journals.

National Strength and Conditioning Association (NSCA), P.O. Box 81410, Lincoln, NE 68501, (403) 472-3000

The NSCA is made up of professional coaches, athletic trainers, physical therapists, sports medicine physicians, and sports science researchers. The group promotes the total conditioning of athletes to a level of optimum performance, with the belief that a better conditioned athlete not only performs better but is less prone to injury. The NSCA sanctions national, regional, state, and local clinics and workshops and distributes several publications to members.

North American Network of Women Runners (NANWR), P.O. Box 719, Bala Cynwyd, PA 19004, (215) 668-9886

The NANWR is made up of female runners,

fitness participants, racers, health professionals, women in sports, and women concerned about opportunities for health, fitness, and sports. The NANWR strives to obtain money that will make athletic careers, physical fitness, and good health accessible to women internationally. The group holds low-cost women's workouts with child care in various community, school, and business facilities. The group also publishes a quarterly newsletter.

President's Council on Physical Fitness and Sports, Washington, DC 20201, (202) 755-7478

The council conducts a public-service advertising program and cooperates with governmental and private groups to promote the development of physical fitness leadership, facilities, and programs. It produces educational materials on exercise, school physical education programs, sports, and physical fitness for youth, adults, and the elderly. Most states have a chapter of this organization identified as the Governor's Council on Physical Fitness and Sports.

Index

sticking point, and training for muscle strength, **29**
storage fat, **11**
strength: 28; *see also,* muscle strength
strength/endurance continuum, 94
stress: and coronary heart disease, 7; and exercise, 18, 52, 53; and hypertension, 6
"stress busters," and exercise, 18
stress fractures, causes and treatment of, 73
"stress" hormones, effect of exercise on, 53
stress test, for medical clearance to begin exercise program, 109, 111–112
stroke volume, and exercise, 25
subcutaneous fatty tissue, and sweating process, 59
submaximum heart-rate limited protocol, exercise stress test, 112
"subprograms," as part of comprehensive fitness program, 83
survival guide, exercise, 99–101
sweat glands: 59; and heat rash, 62; *see also,* sweating
sweating: process, 59, 60, 63; and weight loss, 54
swelling, *see* inflammation
swimming: 19; number of Americans, 1; benefits and costs of, 122; and benefits of cross training, 106–107; and cardiac health, 47
sympathetic nervous system, and exercise, 7
systolic blood pressure: 43, **44;** effect of exercise on, 7, 45

T

target heart rate, 89, 90
target weight, 15
technique, improper, and injuries, 72, 115
technology: and equipment, 2–3; and inactivity, 5

teenagers, *see* adolescents
tennis: 19; benefits and costs of, 122; and cardiac health, 47
thallium scan, and testing for exercise fitness, 112
thermoregulatory processes: **59,** 60; and exercising in cold weather, 66, 68–69; and exercising in hot weather, 63
thinking process, effect of exercise on, 52
tissue plasminogen activator, and exercise, 27
TPA, *see* tissue plasminogen activator
training: **24;** proper approach to, 35–38; for altering body composition, 35; for cardiovascular fitness, 28; concept of, 25–26, 28–35; cross, 2, 18, 106–107; for flexibility, 33–35; risk of injury from, 69–75, 79, 81; for muscular endurance, 32–33; for muscular strength, 28–32
training effect, **25–26**
training loads, for muscular strength, 29
treatment, of injuries, 73–79
triathlons, 2
triglycerides, and coronary heart disease, **45–46**
Tylenol, 78

U

Universal, 31
unreasonable expectations, and goal setting, 113, 115

V

variable resistance exercise, and training for muscle strength, 31
variety: in exercise programs, and preventing boredom, 119, 130, 133–134; *see also,* cross training
VO$_2$ max, **24–25**

W

walking: 2, 19; number of Americans, 1; benefits and costs of, 122; and cardiac health, 47; example of, program, 36–38; sample, program for weight control, 128; test for, 37
warm-up: **73,** 84–85; and preventing aches, 73
water aerobics, 2
weight: control, and health, 48, 50–51, 53, 124; and health, 10–16; and risk of heatstroke, 62
weight control: and health, 48, 50–51, 53; influence of frequency of exercise on, 124; sample exercise program for, 128
weight loads, and programs for muscular strength and endurance, 94, 96, 103
weight training: benefits and costs of, 122; and body composition, 35; developing program for, 94–98, 103; for muscular endurance, 32; for muscular strength, 28–32; personal plan for, 125; and women, 3
weight-loss suits, and common exercise myths, 54
weights, hand, 2
wellness, **4**
whirlpools, *see* heat
wind, and exercising in cold weather, 68
winter, exercising during, 65–69
women: 3, 9; and effect of exercise on cancer of reproductive system, 41; and heart disease, 17; percentage of body fat of, 14
workload, and maintenance of exercise programs, 130

Z

zippers, and dressing to exercise in cold weather, 67

Page 2 Reprinted with permission of *University of California, Berkeley Wellness Letter.* Copyright © Health Letter Associates, 1991. Page 7 Reprinted with permission from *Healthline.* Page 9 Reprinted with permission of *University of California, Berkeley Wellness Letter.* Copyright © Health Letter Associates, 1991. Page 17 Copyright © 1989 by Gruner & Jahr USA Publishing. Reprinted from *Parents* magazine by permission. Page 23 Reprinted with permission of *University of California, Berkeley Wellness Letter.* Copyright © Health Letter Associates, 1991. Page 27 Reprintd with permission of *Johns Hopkins Medical Letter, Health After 50.* Copyright © MedLetter Associates, 1991. Page 36 Copyright © 1991 by Consumers Union of the United States, Inc., Yonkers, NY 10703. Reprinted by permission from *Consumer Reports on Health/Consumer Reports Health Letter,* August 1991. Page 41 By Deborah Franklin. Reprinted from *In Health.* Copyright © 1988. Page 47 From *Newsweek,* Special Advertising Section (1989). Copyright © 1988, Newsweek, Inc. All rights reserved. Reprinted by permission. Page 49 By Valerie Fahey. Reprinted from *In Health.* Copyright © 1988. Page 52 Reprinted with permission from *Psychology Today* magazine. Copyright © 1988 by Sussex Publishers, Inc. Page 54 Copyright © 1991 by Consumers Union of the United States, Inc., Yonkers, NY 10703. Reprinted by permission from *Consumer Reports on Health/Consumer Reports Health Letter,* August 1991. Page 61 Copyright © 1988 by The New York Times Company. Reprinted by permission. Page 67 Reprinted with permission of *University of California, Berkeley Wellness Letter.* Copyright © Health Letter Associates, 1991. Page 72 Reprinted with permission of *University of California, Berkeley Wellness Letter.* Copyright © Health Letter Associates, 1991. Page 76 Reprinted with permission of *University of California, Berkeley Wellness Letter.* Copyright © Health Letter Associates, 1991. Page 80 Special reprint permission granted by *Current Health 2,* published by Weekly Reader Corporation. Copyright © 1990 by Weekly Reader Corporation. *Current Health* is a federally registered trademark of Weekly Reader Corporation. Page 95 Copyright © 1989 by The New York Times Company. Reprinted by permission. Page 99 Reprinted with permission of *University of California, Berkeley Wellness Letter.* Copyright © Health Letter Associates, 1991. Page 106 Reprinted with permission of *University of California, Berkeley Wellness Letter.* Copyright © Health Letter Associates, 1991. Page 111 Reprinted with permission of *Johns Hopkins Medical Letter, Health After 50.* Copyright © Health Letter Associates, 1991. Page 114 Reprinted from *Better Health* with permission. Page 122 Copyright © 1991 by The Kiplinger Washington Editors Inc. Reprinted with permission. Page 129 From *American Health* magazine. Copyright © 1988 by James M. Rippe.